"Insightful and inspiring, Kristy, Sue, and DeAnn take the reader on an often witty yet always poignant tour of hope."

~Donna VanLiere, NY Times best-selling author and speaker

"Wow ... such a breath of fresh air! Incredibly anointed authors coming together to point us toward a victorious biblical mindset for so many of our real life tensions. This book inspires us to have a mindset saturated in Jesus who is the only hope; a confident expectation of a better tomorrow based on the character and promises of Jesus. Dive in. Be empowered. Be equipped. Be encouraged."

~Chris & Holly Brown, Speakers/Authors/Pastors of The Well Church, Columbia, TN/ Radio Host

"Hope comes in many shapes and sizes, too many to count and certainly no one-size-fits all. In the lovely new devotional, from authors Kristy Ensor, Sue Mohr, and DeAnn Starling, hope is served up in all its various expanse. Whether you're married or single, with children or without, this collection will encourage each woman who reads it to fix her eyes on the only one who provides true hope, our Lord and Savior, Jesus Christ."

~Katie Battistelli, Author of The God Dare and Growing Great Kids

"*Hope is* ... an encouraging breath of fresh air during what can be described as a turbulent season for us all. The honest, raw, and gritty real-life stories of endurance and trust in the Lord will indeed bring you hope and lead you to the true source of peace that passes understanding. These gifted ladies will have you crying one moment and belly laughing the next. The perfect devotional for anyone who could use a deep dose of hope"

~Lyn Carr, MAR/Hospice Chaplain

"Life can be hard, and hope can feel so far away at time. *Hope is …* offers us reminders that, even in the midst of uncertainty, fear, doubt, and the unknown, we can find peace and comfort in God and the hope He offers. Through sharing their own stories and experiences, our mom, Sue Mohr, and her friends, Kristy and DeAnn, have written a roadmap to search for the hope of Jesus in all circumstances. We are so lucky to have grown up hearing and applying these encouraging words and stories from our mama and can't wait for the rest of the world to experience her creative wisdom."

~Amber/Sarah/Julia, EVERLIFE

"A guiding light that illuminates the path through life's challenges. Messages of real-life experiences that inspire one to hold on to the hope that brings forth the desires of our hearts. Readers feel understood, courageous, and equipped for battle. The writers are real hope dealers."

~Krista Anderson, Founder & CEO of Healthy On The Go/ESSTAR – esstar.us

HOPE IS ...

Hope is . . .

Kristy Ensor, Sue Mohr, and

DeAnn Starling

Bold Vison Books
PO Box 2011
Friendswood, Texas 77549

Copyright ©Sue Mohr, Kristy Ensor, DeAnn Starling 2022
ISBN978-1946708-79-3
Library of Congress Control Number 2022945003
All rights reserved.
Published by Bold Vision Books, PO Box 2011, Friendswood, Texas 77549
www.boldvisionbooks.com
Published in cooperation with Macey Howell, Jones Literary Agency

Cover Design by Amber Wiegand-Buckley, Bareface Creative
Interior design by kae Creative Solutions
Published in the United States of America.

Who We Are

Hope Is . . . was written by good friends Kristy Ensor, Sue Mohr, and DeAnn Starling. The authors created a group called *The Crooked Crown Writing Society* in a small town outside of Nashville, Tennessee. They offer support by straightening one another's crowns when they begin to fall. They wear proverbial *crowns* because they are daughters of the King of Kings, the Most High God. The group's primary purpose is to foster creativity and provide accountability for their various writing projects while glorifying God and inspiring others.

"Hope collects the tattered pieces of our lives, stitching them
into something beautiful. It gives us courage and strength,
lifting us up to a place where we can soar."

– The Crooked Crown Writing Society

Dedication

To all those searching for hope. May you find it in these pages. Most importantly, may you find it in the One who is our greatest source of hope.

Table of Contents

Preface

What is hope?

A wish? An expectation? A feeling?

No matter how we define it, most of us spend our entire lives searching for it.

"I hope I get accepted into a great college."

"I hope I get married."

"I hope I make a lot of money."

"I hope I make my family proud."

"I hope I am successful."

We feel hopeful if our circumstances work out the way we want or if people cooperate with our plans.

But . . .

What if that doesn't happen?

Ironically, we began writing this book on hope about six weeks before the world shut down due to the Covid-19 pandemic. People lost jobs, family members, and peace of mind. Political and racial tensions reached a breaking point.

Where was hope then?

The three of us discussed this each week as we wrote. We all had felt hopeless at times in our lives. Sickness, death, and hurts had threatened to defeat us. The common thread that sustained us was our faith. We had finally realized our hope would never be found in our ever-changing circumstances. Instead, it would be anchored by a never-changing God.

God has shown us hope at the deathbed of loved ones, in high-risk pregnancies, and in the depths of depression. Sometimes His lessons show up in somber situations, while others are revealed through disastrous home makeovers, torturous diet plans, or even a hero with a toilet plunger. We still don't claim to be experts in hope, but we did the math, and the three of us have over one hundred and fifty years of combined experience in searching for it.

Our desire is for you to find hope and maybe even a little laughter as you read how we've struggled to move forward with confidence in God's plan even when our own plans fail. Our prayer is that you will be inspired to look beyond your circumstances and find your ultimate hope in the promises of God and the gift of His Son, Jesus.

Chapter 1

Discovering Hope in a Hopeless World

Faith Takes the Plunge

Kristy

*Let us hold on unswervingly to the hope we profess,
for he who promised is faithful. Hebrews 10:23*

When I was growing up, my family took vacations to Carolina beaches. One summer, we stayed in an oceanfront condominium with a beautiful view. It was a picture-perfect day filled with swimming in the waves, building majestic sandcastles, and having a blast while playing card games. At least it was fun until we managed to clog the toilet ... without a plunger in sight.

We called the building maintenance number. No answer.

The condo only had one bathroom, and I quickly grew frustrated. I was too young to drive but remembered a nearby store within walking distance. I asked my parents if my little brother and I could walk there to buy a plunger. They agreed, and off we went.

Upon arrival, we were briefly sidetracked by the candy aisle. Because what kid wouldn't be, right? We picked out a few sweet treats and continued with our mission. Thankfully, the store had plungers. I grabbed one, and we went to pay. I marched back to the condo with my brother by my side, purse thrown over my shoulder, with the bag of candy in one hand and the plunger in the other.

Once we returned, Dad took care of the plunging and got the toilet back in working order. Since I'd bought the plunger, I felt like a superhero who saved the day, proud of myself for taking action to remedy the situation.

Years passed, and I eventually married and had my own family. Having heard the story, my husband surprised me with a Precious Moments figurine. I wasn't a collector, but I could see this one was special. This ceramic little girl, painted in the PM signature pastels, had rollers in her hair and an unmistakably proud, purposeful stride as she seemed to march . . . with a plunger in her hand. The box bore the title "Faith Takes the Plunge." Oh, did that gift make me smile.

That sweet little doll figurine, plunger held high, still sits on my nightstand. Not only does it bring fond memories of our family vacation, but it's a wonderful reminder about faith.

Sometimes our faith takes a plunge, doesn't it? Thankfully, God is the real hero of our stories, giving us strength to carry on, and providing tools in our tool belts to help us overcome. Sometimes that tool happens to come in the form of a plunger. Our faith can be strengthened when God gives us tools to navigate life.

He also provides us with hope to endure life's difficult situations. Whether it's as simple as being frustrated by a clogged toilet or something much worse, there's always hope. That hope carries us through each day. Jesus comes to us, even in the darkest hours, and He brings hope. He is that hope.

Do things work out how we think they will? Sometimes. But not always, and that's okay because hope in Jesus is having confidence that He remains faithful. It is the certainty that Jesus' purposes will be fulfilled. Let's praise Him for giving us strength to carry on, tools to overcome, and the courage to face each day. It's safe to hold onto the promises of God and the hope He brings.

Dear Lord,

Thank You for giving me the hope and strength to carry on during tough times. Please help me to live by faith and remain hopeful—even during life's adversities. Amen.

Growing in Hope

1. What is one "precious moment" or special memory you hold dear from childhood?

2. How did God help carry you through a difficult situation?

3. Do you live by faith and have hope in the Lord? Why or why not? Please explain.

Minus the Less

Sue

*But those who hope in the Lord will renew
their strength. They will soar on wings like
eagles; they will run and not grow weary, they
will walk and not be faint.*

Isaiah 40:31

Hope. Such a tiny word. Yet it has the power to hold the world's very existence in its hand. To live life happily and "expect with confidence" provides a skip in our daily step. But when hope is absent from our lives, we feel powerless. Unable to escape our shadows. You know which ones I mean—those dark figures that are bigger than we are. They skulk around, following our every move. Attaching themselves to us night and day, all the while blocking the light in our life.

I've struggled with the absence of hope during various times throughout my life. Have you ever walked into a room and exclaimed, "Woah, it's dark in here." only to discover your sunglasses were still on your face?

Herein lies the problem. Without light, we cannot see. It's plain and simple. We stumble around with perpetual blindfolds over our minds' eyes. Unable to avoid the pitfalls that surround us. We become exhausted. Rest eludes us. Not a break is in sight as we find ourselves in a never-ending race against time. Tripping over everything life brings our way. Hopelessness becomes the word of the day.

When hope arrives, though, it is akin to the light the sun provides. It brightens and brings warmth to our paths. Allowing us to clearly see what is right in front of us. Shedding light on what was behind us and, more than anything, opening a clear view of what the future holds.

Hope transforms us. It's like when a snake sheds its skin and underneath there is a fresh, new layer. A snake doesn't stop to pick up the old skin and take it with him. He leaves it behind, never looking back. You see, it makes the utmost sense, because it no longer fits. Its usefulness is over. When hope arrives in our lives, hopelessness is like that old skin. It is dried up and useless. Once we get a taste of how amazing hope feels and marvel at how well it fits, we no longer want to put on that old covering. That would be silly.

Isaiah 40:31 lays this out so eloquently for us. I've always loved that personification—*They will soar on wings like eagles.* The unique thing about an eagle's wings is that they are long and wide, helping the bird soar and glide with little effort. Hope does that. We no longer need to scratch and crawl through life wondering when the next break will happen. Instead, we hope. We stand solid on the fact that God is our hope. Gliding is our new method of transportation. Our former cumbersome and arduous stride is now replaced with a smooth and graceful stroll.

What if we just stepped out of the way every time "less-ness" tried to attach itself to our hope? I believe it would disappear, like a puff of smoke. Poof. Gone. Present for only a moment, but then gone the next. For without our attention, without us feeding it, without a backward glance, it loses its power. Hopelessness can't exist without a host.

We don't need to search for hope constantly. It is within grasp right now. All we need to do is reach out, put it on, and get ready to soar.

Dear Father,

Thank You for wrapping up the gift of hope and leaving it where we can easily find it. Your gift is wrapped so beautifully with Your love. That's plain to see, for every time we even tug on the ribbon, our hope is renewed. Amen.

Growing in *Hope*

1. Describe a time when hopelessness was part of your wardrobe, only for you to look back now and see that God had a new outfit, in your size, ready and waiting for you.

2. How has hope changed the light on your path?

3. What emotions do the phrase "they will run and not grow weary, they will walk and not be faint" evoke in you?

Seeing Hope

DeAnn

*I pray that the eyes of your heart may be
enlightened in order that you may know the
hope to which he has called you, the riches of his
glorious inheritance in his holy people, and his
incomparably great power for us who believe. That
power is the same as the mighty strength he exerted
when he raised Christ from the dead …*

Ephesians 1:18-20

There is no cure.

The words on my computer screen were clear, yet I reread them
several times, hoping to find an exception to this harsh reality.

My dad had been sick for about a year, and every specialist my parents visited seemed baffled by his condition. Finally, a cardiologist decided to take a biopsy of my dad's heart and send the tissue to Mayo Clinic. Their doctors diagnosed AL amyloidosis, a rare, terminal disease. My parents' doctor delivered the bad news and suggested hospice care. Hoping he was wrong, I flipped on my computer to search for answers. And there were the words. "Incurable." "Fatal."

It is hard to know what to say to someone who has just been told there is no hope—at least not on this earth.

I knew my dad had his ultimate hope in Jesus, yet I could not see past the immediate despair.

I felt compelled to give my dad hope for a cure. After researching for hours on my computer, I found an expert in London who had experienced some success in treating one patient with AL amyloidosis. One. But that was enough.

I sent the doctor a quick email explaining the situation and asking for help. He agreed to work with my dad's doctors.

When I told my dad the news, I could see his spirits lift immediately. We spent the day talking about this new plan.

A glimmer. A tiny thread of hope. That's all we needed.

However, the next morning, my dad went into a coma. Within hours, we realized he would not awaken this side of heaven. The date was June 18, his birthday. Instead of planning his birthday party, we would be planning a funeral.

But then the Lord spoke to me. What better birthday gift could my dad receive than to see Jesus?

I prayed for my dad to enter heaven on his birthday if he had to die. I needed some assurance that God was still in control in this hopelessness.

By 11:00 p.m., I wondered if Dad would linger for days or weeks. I was sure I would not survive the inevitable, and I begged God for strength. A few minutes later, my dad began to breathe sporadically. My mom ran to find a nurse, and I knew. This was it.

I told my dad as passionately as I could, "You have been the best father. You can go to heaven and be with Jesus. I will take care of everything here." At 11:15 p.m., the moment I finished speaking, Dad drew his last breath. He made it to heaven on his birthday.

For years, I have struggled to put into words what I experienced at that moment. Something holy. So powerful and overwhelming, I would never have the words to describe it. I didn't exactly see my dad enter heaven, but I felt it. Just as certain as anything I have ever witnessed.

I was reminded of Paul's words in Ephesians. "I pray that the eyes of your heart may be enlightened in order that you may know the hope to which he has called you, the riches of his glorious inheritance in his holy people, and his incomparably great power for us who believe" (1:18-19).

That was it. I saw heaven with "the eyes of my heart." At death's door, I knew hope. Real hope, not just the miniscule hope of a miracle cure on earth. I saw God's power. Not just any power, but "power that is the same as the mighty strength he exerted when he raised Christ from the dead" (1:19-20).

I had tried to offer my dad a sliver of hope in life, but he gave me a glimpse in death of the vastness of our ultimate hope in heaven. From that moment on, I knew I would not only survive my dad's death but be empowered by God with His mighty strength to face any challenges in my life.

Dear God,

Thank You for the ultimate hope You give us in Christ. Open the eyes of our hearts when we can't see past our circumstances. Strengthen us with the same power that raised Christ from the dead. Amen.

Growing in *Hope*

1. What situation in your life has seemed hopeless and beyond your control? How did you try to fix it yourself?

2. Can you remember a time in your life when you survived a tragedy? Explain how you found hope in that circumstance.

3. How has God used His power to encourage you?

Chapter 2

Replacing Worry with Faith

Don't Look So Down

Kristy

Humble yourselves, therefore, under God's mighty hand, that he may lift you up in due time. Cast all your anxiety on him because he cares for you. 1 Peter 5:6-7

I'm what you might call a natural born worrier. I know worrying doesn't do one bit of good, but sometimes I do it anyway. Old habits die hard. The older I get, the less I worry, though. Because through the years, I've witnessed God's faithfulness and trustworthiness. I've grown in my spiritual walk and now realize I can fully depend on Him without any doubts. He's got this. Whatever the "it" might be, He's got it. I try to trust Him more and worry less, but that wasn't always the case. I distinctly remember being anxious about a specific situation when in middle school.

"Don't look so down, kid. You've got me for a teacher." Those were the first words my seventh-grade teacher, Ms. Cansler, said to me. Of all the teachers at the school, she was not my first pick. Let me clarify. I did not want her as a teacher. We had open classrooms, and her room was near my sixth-grade science class the year prior. I remembered all too well her loud voice carrying down the hall. She seemed strict, and I dreaded even the thought of having her as a teacher. I worried about it.

To my dismay, I ended up getting her for homeroom and Language Arts. There must have been a troubled look on my face when Ms. Cansler walked by my desk on that first day of school. However, when she smiled, patted me on the back, and spoke those words over me, "Don't look so down kid. You've got me for a teacher," it lifted my spirits.

In Proverbs, Solomon wrote, "Anxiety weighs down the heart, but a kind word cheers it up" (Proverbs 12:25). Ms. Cansler's kind words put me at ease that day. They brought comfort and cheered me up.

I soon realized she wasn't so bad after all. I had misjudged her. She was strict. That part was true. It turned out, though, that she was a wonderful teacher. She encouraged me to write and told me I had a gift. She once gave our class an assignment to create a poetry book, and I fell in love with writing even more.

Ms. Cansler ended up being one of my favorite teachers. God used her to make a positive impact on my life. I'd worried for no reason.

I still have days when I stress. I'm human. However, being stressed out interferes with our faith. We must strive to engage in faith rather than be wrecked by worry. When I hand my troubles over, trusting the Lord with my life and everything in it, I am better off. Worry defeats us while faith strengthens us. Worrying is a quick way to nowhere. Having faith is the best way to find peace under God's mighty hand.

One morning, I was having my quiet time when suddenly I felt compelled to turn to Psalm 23. I've read the twenty-third Psalm many, many times. I'm very familiar with it, even memorized it as a kid. So why did I need to read it? What was the sudden urgency? I turned there in my Bible and stopped dead in my tracks. I couldn't get past the first verse. The King James version reads, "The LORD is my shepherd; I shall not want." Mic drop moment. The Holy Spirit was telling me not to worry. I. Shall. Not. Want. The New International Version reads, "The LORD is my shepherd, I lack nothing." Nothing. We lack nothing because He takes care of us. We can turn all our worries over to God.

I encourage you to cast your anxieties on Him. He is worthy of trust. He cares about your every need, and your worries are safe with Him.

Dear Lord,

Thank You for caring for my every need. Please take away worrisome thoughts and replace them with Your perfect peace. Help me to have enough faith to put my total trust in You. Amen.

Overcoming Worry

1. Are you worried about something now? Write it down.

2. What would it look like to trust Jesus enough to turn that worry over to him?

3. How would your life change if you worried less and trusted Him more?

Why Worry?

Sue

Worry weighs a person down; an encouraging word
cheers a person up. Proverbs 12:25 (NLT)

When I open the Bible and read scripture, it takes me down so many roads. Just like the story lines in a good book, God's word evokes emotion, feelings, and deep thoughts. It contains high roads and low roads, scenes filled with chaos and war, along with electrifying moments of life and death. More than anything, though, I've found it provides focused direction and guidance. I sure need that on a daily basis.

One of my favorite books in the Bible is Proverbs. It's a great "if you do this, then this could happen" kind of guide. A guide that gives you a view into how your future decisions will play out.

Life happens, and along with it, stuff happens. I've committed my lion's share of poor decisions, along with finding myself in situations beyond my control. There have been financial issues, family problems, broken relationships, and so much more. As I allowed the pain of each of these to permeate and spin deep within my mind and soul on a continual loop, they soon resulted in a negative common denominator called worry.

Worry is like mold. It creeps up and grows in places that are hidden from the human eye. Then, before you know it, it is mushrooming out of control. Worry takes over, and the spores feed on and devour everything in its path. When its presence is revealed, it's next to impossible to get rid of without investing in a costly intervention.

Let's take a look at Proverbs 12:25. The first part states, "Worry weighs a person down." Ugh. I sure know that to be true. When I close my eyes and get a mental picture of worry, he looks like a huge, taloned beast, trying to gain a permanent hold on my back. He is never satiated, consuming everything his hands can reach. His weight, his constant movement, takes me off balance. While trying to walk a straight line, I trip, and every muscle in my body is taxed to pure exhaustion. Sound familiar?

But true to the vein of Proverbs, the next line is where hope arises. "An encouraging word cheers a person up." That right there, my friends, is a powerful mold killer. A solution to get rid of that beast once and for all.

Start with yourself. You deserve the first encouraging words because you are a child of the Most High King. Now work your way down. Let it trickle to your family, your friends, your friend's friends, neighbors, acquaintances, and so on. Before you know it, worry has lost its power. It has run out of fuel. Its life source has been extinguished. Hope can now take its place.

Then a domino effect begins. One encouraging word touches another that touches another that touches many. With worry out of the way and encouragement taking center stage, what a different life we will live.

Dear Lord,

Help us to replace worry with hope. Hope in You. Knowing full well that You have our back. May we lean on Your encouragement, finding it at every turn while we seek Your face. Help us to speak kindly of ourselves, so we can encourage others. Amen.

Overcoming Worry

1. Has worry ever spread to the nooks and crannies in your life? Name a time when hope replaced it.

2. What are three ways you can eliminate worry from your life right now?

3. Write down ten words that are the opposite of worry. How can you apply those words to your life?

Giving Up Worry

DeAnn

Do not be anxious about anything, but in every situation, by prayer and petition, with thanksgiving, present your requests to God. And the peace of God, which transcends all understanding, will guard your hearts and your minds in Christ Jesus. Philippians 4:6-7

For years, I have suffered from a candy addiction. Specifically, milk chocolate M&M's. Without peanuts. Do not mess with perfection, please.

M&M's have seen me through many of my most difficult life circumstances. When I had to pull all-nighters in college while studying for finals, this sweet candy gave me the sugar high I needed to persevere. When my babies screamed for hours with colic, M&M's provided my continued comfort. When my husband was hospitalized with septic shock, I had several pound bags lying securely beside me in the ICU.

Imagine my surprise when my husband and I decided to give up something for Lent a few years ago, and I chose M&M's. This had to be a calling from God because I would never have willingly parted with my favorite candy without divine intervention.

That Lent was the longest 40 days of my life. I have little willpower on my own. I needed a plan, so I banned M&M's from our house, substituted different desserts, and chewed gum. I put pictures of people who ate healthy on the refrigerator. I struggled. I prayed. I may have even cried, just imagining the smooth, satisfying taste of my favorite chocolate candy.

At the end of Lent, I anxiously tore into a huge bag of M&M's, but a funny thing happened. They didn't taste as good. I even bought a second bag just to make sure, but the result was the same. For the first time ever, I could take them or leave them.

A year later, I noticed I was spending a lot of my day feeling anxious, so I decided to give up worry for Lent. If stepping away from M&M's had made them less appealing, could I become less inclined to worry?

A few weeks later, the Covid-19 pandemic hit our country, and worry was the topic of almost every conversation. I knew I was in over my head trying to give up worry on my own, so I studied scripture for inspiration. I discovered the Bible doesn't just tell us not to worry; it gives us specific instructions and steps to take. We can't simply shrug off worry. That would be like me telling myself to just stop eating M&M's without having a plan. We actually have to participate in the process of not worrying.

Paul tells us in Philippians 4 not to worry, but we are then told to pray and present our requests to God and be thankful. We must pray, tell God about our worries, and thank Him for all He has done for us. Then the peace of God will guard our hearts and minds.

I decided to follow these directions. Each time a worry about the pandemic or my children or our future came to mind, I immediately stopped to pray, discuss the problem with God, turn the problem over to Him, and be thankful. Since that time, I can honestly say I have somewhat lost my "taste" for worry. Worries haven't automatically disappeared, but I now try my best to hand them over to God.

And just as I released my addiction to M&M's, I no longer feel the need to keep a one-pound bag of worry beside me to get through life's challenges.

Dear God,

Thank You for promising Your peace in this life, no matter what the circumstances. Help me turn my worries over to You when I am anxious. Thank You for providing an action plan for me to find peace. Amen.

Overcoming **Worry**

1. What situations have caused you to worry?

2. How have you tried to cope with worry? What did it look like when God entered the plan

3. How might your life look differently if you prayed, thanked God, and turned your concerns over to Him all the time? When can you start this habit?

Chapter 3

Finding the Greater Love

The Love I Never Knew I Needed

Kristy

A new command I give you: Love one another. As
I have loved you, so you must love one another.
John 13:34

Most little girls tend to dream about marrying Prince Charming, having a fairytale wedding, and living happily ever after. Some also dream of having kids. I was not that girl. When I pictured my future, it looked quite different. I imagined myself being single and thought I'd focus solely on a successful career as a writer or news journalist. In fact, I dreamed of being a news anchor in a thriving metropolis and hoped to be the next Barbara Walters. I wanted to interview many fascinating people like she did. I also thought I'd live in a condo and bike to work. My dreams were to live it up, enjoy big city life, and relish in the freedoms of my singleness.

I majored in communications with a journalism emphasis. Once I obtained my bachelor's degree, I thought I was well on my way to achieving the career goals I'd been dreaming of all those years. I was young and naive. My plans quickly changed after I happened to work in a summer enrichment program serving students with special needs. I fell in love with the kids.

My co-workers told me I'd missed my calling and should've majored in special education. Just like that, I switched gears and started serving children with autism and other learning differences. Later I decided to attend graduate school and work toward a master's degree in special education. I met my husband the first day on campus, and this was the beginning of our love story. The running joke is that I never finished my master's, but I received my "Mrs." instead.

Two years after meeting Ken, the love of my life, we had a lovely outdoor ceremony at a farmhouse surrounded by beautiful flower gardens. Our wedding and honeymoon were special and topped with perfect weather. Our marriage was off to a great start. Several months later, we found out I was pregnant.

Sadly, we experienced the sorrow of a miscarriage shortly thereafter. We knew my chances of having a baby were slim due to an underlying medical condition. Thankfully, about six months after the miscarriage, we received the good news that I was pregnant a second time. This time we celebrated the joy of having a sweet baby boy to love.

I have watched God go before me in many circumstances. I didn't throw away my original dreams for the future. Instead, God transformed my dreams and plans. Today I cannot fathom my life without the love of my husband and son. The Lord allowed me to trade my big city dreams for small-town life with a family I adore.

Having the love of my heavenly Father and the love of my family are my greatest gifts. I learned what the command "love one another" really means. To me, it's being present and showing up for my family, friends, and sometimes even strangers. It's loving without conditions. It's putting the needs of others in front of my own. To me, it means exhibiting Christ-like behavior so that our love sets us apart.

I'm thankful for the blessing of my family. I have the love I never knew I needed. We might not always get what we think we want, but God is faithful to go before us and meet our needs. God's love knows no bounds. Oh, how He loves us so much.

Dear Lord,

Thank You for going before me and meeting my needs. Even when my dreams don't go as I envision, Your love and plans are always better. I praise You for giving me people to love. Help me remember Your ways are higher than mine. I love You Father, and thanks for loving me so much. Amen.

Growing in *Love*

1. Did your childhood dreams come true? Please explain.

2. Has a dream turned out differently than you thought it would?

3. How has God met your needs in unexpected ways? Did you feel His love?

What Kind of Friend Are You?

Sue

Greater love has no one than this: to lay down one's life for one's friends. John 15:13

What if someone asked me, "Would you lay down your life for your husband?" My answer would be, "Of course, yes." Would I lay down my life for my daughters and grand-littles? Inexplicably, yes. But would I lay down my life for a friend? Hmmm. I must be honest, I'm not so sure.

Jesus didn't hesitate like I just did. He came down from heaven to walk in human shoes. This was the story of God, who became man so He could lay down His life for His friends. This wasn't just a flippant decision. As flesh and blood, He knew struggles, became tired, got angry, suffered pain, dealt with ridicule, experienced beatings, was hated and then murdered. Even with all this, He chose to lay His life down, paying the ultimate sacrifice. He did this because He loves me. He is my friend. Knew me before I even took my first breath. Loves me more than my parents ever could. His desire is for me not to perish into nothingness, but to spend eternity in glory with His Father.

Left to my own devices, I am clearly unable to make this happen on my own. My friend, Jesus, stood in front of me when the bullets of life came whizzing past. Like the superhero He is, He caught each one. He took my shame, my guilt, my sin, my pain and rolled it all up in a tight little bundle. Then He put it on His back and began the long, excruciating walk to the cross.

But would I do that for a friend? I wish my immediate answer was a resounding yes. Jesus didn't doubt His decision. I do take comfort, though, in that one moment, on the night before his death, when He asked His heavenly Father to take that cup from Him (Luke 22:42). Instead of this taking away from His deity or the sacredness of who He was, it actually gives me hope.

I've often told my clients that in our humanness, we need to give ourselves grace for our first thoughts. They just happen. The second thought, though, that's where the lies start to feel like truth, and the enemy wants us to believe them. Those are the ones that need to be taken captive.

Jesus had that first thought. A human thought. Yet He, in all His glory, covered that with a promise. A promise that He would lay down His life for me, for you, His friends. Because I am a human. Because I doubt. Because I hesitate, this means even more to me. I don't take His ultimate sacrifice of love for granted, and I'm thankful that my friendship with Jesus is eternal.

Dear Lord,

I wish there was another human phrase to express my "thank you." Those words just never seem to be enough. Your sacrifice is everything to me. You saved me from myself, from my own destruction, from an eternity without You and Your Father. Your love for me is beyond anything I can know this side of heaven. Thank You for being my friend. Amen.

Growing in *Love*

1. Think about the ultimate decision of love that Jesus made. Where would you be if He hadn't?

2. Have you ever found yourself in a situation where you had to choose between yourself and your friend? What did that feel like? What would you change, if anything, if you had the opportunity?

3. What does your "thank you" to Jesus look like today?

Loving without Expectations

DeAnn

We love because he first loved us.

1 John 4:19

Her words struck fear in my heart.

"Mom, can I bring home three friends from college for fall break?" my daughter asked innocently.

On a good day, this would cause hours of mild panic, days of frantic cleaning, and weeks expertly hiding our miscellaneous, ever-expanding piles of *stuff* in closets and under beds.

But now? We had bought new bedding for my daughter's room a year earlier but failed to paint the lime green walls that no longer matched. And the bathrooms? All the flooring had been ripped up after a flood the previous year and had not been replaced. The walls were covered in various paint samples. There was no way I could let these girls see the mess in our house. But I didn't have the heart to turn her down.

"Sure. Just tell them not to expect much," I said, wondering how in the world I could pull this off—a miracle makeover if there ever was one.

The second I hung up the phone, I went to work. I painted a bedroom and a bathroom in two days. I bought accessories and curtains. I purchased new rugs to cover the sub-flooring from the flood fiasco. I deep cleaned. I baked with record speed. I cried from exhaustion. I was literally vacuuming the last room when the girls drove into our driveway.

The girls had a blast. They spent so much time touring in nearby Nashville, they hardly noticed the home makeover.

After they left, I collapsed on the sofa, so proud I had pulled off a major feat in record time. A few minutes later, the phone rang, and I heard our daughter asking my husband to answer some questions about a school project.

"What was that about?" I asked.

"Oh, nothing really," he answered. Hardly convincing.

"No, seriously, tell me," I said.

"She's writing a paper in her class about the person she most admires, and she asked me some questions about myself," he replied.

"Wait, What? You? You are the person she most admires?" I yelled.

I thought back to the shopping, painting, cleaning, cooking, and decorating.

"But you watched football while I did all this. How can you be the most admired? Isn't the one who works the hardest the most admired?" I ranted.

Now normally, I would be proud that our daughter admired her dad. I even try to encourage it on my good days. But this just seemed so ... so unfair.

I had to go sit in a hot bath to talk it out with God. And there I realized—Isn't that exactly how I act toward Him?

"Lord, I will teach this Bible study, lead a mission trip, give my tithe, and sometimes try to love my enemies, but can I please still be recognized? Can I get my name on an award or at least get a pat on the back? Can I be the most admired?"

Somehow during my bathtub soak, God showed me I wasn't serving my daughter out of love. I was expecting a reward. A Mother of the Year plaque at a minimum.

Yet God says we should love because He first loved us. Period. The End. We should be so filled to overflowing with thankfulness because of His Great Love that we can't help but express love to others.

Today, I can look back at that moment as a family memory that makes us all smile. I'll ask, "Remember when I wasn't the most admired?" and we all burst out laughing.

I'm thankful the Lord uses everyday circumstances to teach us how to love the way He loves us, even if the lesson does involve painting and scrubbing.

Dear Lord,

Teach me how to love. Help me to be so filled with Your amazing love that I can't help but serve others. Show me that Your great love is all the reward I will ever need. Amen.

Growing in *Love*

1. What do I expect when I serve others? And when I serve God?

2. How can I love better without hoping for recognition or a reward?

3. Picture God's great love for you. How has He loved you without expectations? How have you seen His love for you?

Chapter 4

Embracing Comfort in the Midst of Grief

Hitting Rock Bottom

Kristy

Record my misery; list my tears on your scroll—are they not in your record? Psalm 56:8

According to scripture, God collects our tears and keeps track of them. I can't fathom the number of tears He has from me. I tend to feel deeply, and sometimes the tears just flow. Whether it's a soul-stirring song, a sad movie, or even a touching commercial, I often fight to hold back the tears.

Then there are the all too familiar tears of grief. Grief shows up in many heart-shattering and sometimes unexpected ways. A miscarriage happens. A loved one dies. A close friend walks away. A job goes by the wayside. When losses occur, what remains steadfast is the Lord and His promises. He promised to never leave us or forsake us, and He's always there to help mend our heartbreaks.

I have leaned on Him to get me through numerous sad times. Amid the pain and suffering, God gave me the strength to carry on and gradually healed my grieving heart in every scenario. Psalm 34:18 reads, "The LORD is close to the brokenhearted and saves those who are crushed in spirit." I am so thankful that even when my spirit is crushed, He sweeps in and binds up my wounds. He rescues me.

I am ever so thankful the Lord is always there by our side. He offers much needed comfort, peace, and strength. He is our ultimate rescuer in sorrowful times.

One time when I was suffering a serious bout of depression, I grieved because I'd lost the will to keep living. I felt like giving up. I was hospitalized and received intense medical intervention. I even had to undergo ECT treatments (electroconvulsive therapy) to help my severely depressed state.

When a counselor asked me how I was feeling, I replied with a "woe is me" type answer and expressed my gloom like Eeyore would in Winnie the Pooh. To my surprise, the counselor said, "Well hallelujah sister. Praise the Lord."

I looked at him like he'd lost his ever-loving mind and wondered why he seemed so happy.

He said, "You've finally hit rock bottom. Now there's nowhere else to go but up."

Just then, a ray of sun beamed through the window, and I felt the presence of God. I knew He was there to help me during that painful situation. From that point forward, I started getting better and was soon released from the hospital.

If you are grief-stricken, or hitting rock bottom like I was, I encourage you to turn your eyes toward Jesus. You can run to Him with your pain. Keep looking up. He'll pull you through and help heal you. May God bless you and keep you during the sad seasons in your life.

Dear Lord,

When my heart is heavy with grief, I praise You for lifting my spirits. Thank You for being near the brokenhearted and for comforting me in times of sorrow. Please give me the strength to carry on and a peace that surpasses all understanding. I love You Jesus, and I'm ever so grateful that You love me too, walking alongside me during life's sad times. Amen.

Overcoming *Grief*

1. Think about a time when you experienced grief. What was the root of your sadness?

2. Name a time when you've felt the presence of God during a difficult time. How did He help heal your grieving heart?

3. What have you learned from grief, and how have you moved forward?

The Sting of Grief Uninvited

Sue

May your unfailing love be my comfort ...

Psalm 119:76

Nothing ever prepares us for the loss of a loved one nor for the grief that quickly follows. It's different for everyone. Some of us want the world to stop turning, others stop turning their world, and some bottle it up inside. It affects us from the inside out. We all have a unique reaction when grief comes to us uninvited.

It's been said that grief gets easier as time goes by. From my personal experience, I have to disagree. Grief seems to come when you least expect it, and without intervention it doesn't lose its sting over time as so many well-meaning people will tell you. In fact, the sting seems to deepen, it pierces the surface, and finds deep crevices to enter.

My experience has shown that grief knows where you live, and it lies in wait until the next time it sees fit to invade.

Grief gave me an uninvited visit when Mama went home.

With every new life memory, I've wanted to pick up the phone and tell my mama about it. But I can't. That's when grief shows up time and time again and hits me in the middle of my gut.

Life is different without Mama in it. Every time we celebrate one of her grandchildren's birthdays, I can't help but wish she could see not only how they have grown into such beautiful humans, but I also grieve for my daughters not having Grandma around. I can't rip out pages of my life when grief shows up, though. I've had to learn how to let it come and allow it to be part of my story.

Grief is consistent with all kinds of loss, not just the loss of human life. Divorce, separation from friends and family, broken friendships, loss of a pet or a job, and so much more. We attach words like sorrow, misery, sadness, anguish, distress, while trying to capture and describe this epitome of pain.

God knew we would need to be comforted. He is the Father of compassion. The God of comfort.

Grief is personal, but we don't need to be alone to grieve. God is with us. There is not one part of our story that surprises Him. I believe the words in 2 Corinthians 1:4. He comforts us so that we can comfort others. This is where grief starts to look different. We need comforted. We need to reach out to our heavenly Father for comfort. In turn, we learn His compassion and we begin to comfort others. The pain softens as we walk in this flow. Our grief is still there, but it takes on a different hue.

One day, the grief will dissipate. It may not happen on this side of heaven, but God's ultimate desire is to change our sorrow to joy, our misery to gladness, and our distress to eternal peace with Him.

My prayer for all of us is that when grief knocks at our door, we reach out to someone and ask them to walk us through its visit. We weren't created to live life alone, just as we weren't created to grieve alone.

Dear Lord,

You know our pain. You know our tears when grief enters our lives. Thank You for loving us through it all and for offering Your loving comfort. Amen.

Overcoming *Grief*

1. Can you remember a time when you were filled with grief, just to discover that you weren't alone? Explain.

2. Have you allowed grief to be a part of your story, or are you pushing it away? Why?

3. Take a moment to consider how God has comforted you throughout your life.

Lessons from Grief

DeAnn

Praise be to the God and Father of our Lord Jesus Christ, the Father of compassion and the God of all comfort, who comforts us in all our troubles, so that we can comfort those in any trouble with the comfort we ourselves have received from God. For just as we share abundantly in the sufferings of Christ, so also our comfort abounds through Christ. 2 Corinthians 1:3-5

If there was anything I had tried to avoid in my life, it was grief. Yet there I sat, in a church classroom, surrounded by it.

After my father died, I had to navigate a reality I'd been dreading for decades. To cope, I attended a class on overcoming grief, and the tears flowed. Not only my tears, but the tears of everyone in the room. Tears of a young pregnant girl who desperately wished her mom was alive to help raise the baby. Tears from a woman in her forties whose husband died instantly from a heart attack. Sobs from a young newlywed who lost his wife to cancer.

I learned a lot about grief in that classroom.

First, grief comes in many forms, not just in death. Even though I hadn't called it grief, I had experienced it. Lost friendships. Career disappointments. Illness. Mistakes. Missed opportunities. The list was long.

Second, we are never alone in our grief. We are sustained by "the Father of compassion and the God of all comfort, who comforts us in all our troubles." All our troubles. Whether our troubles are big or small, God is there supporting us.

Third, I learned that even something as devastating as grief can be used for good. It can be a gift, even if it is one we would never choose to open. Grief provides a way to minister to others. After experiencing grief, I had better rapport with those suffering deep losses. Because God has comforted me, I was able to comfort others who were going through similar situations. I could wipe away another's tears just as He would.

The very thing I tried to avoid in life became the best way for me to help others.

I recently reunited with a friend I had not seen in years. She was in a horrific accident ten years ago and is now paralyzed. For hours, we discussed the highs and lows of the past decade. She opened up to me about some of her hardest struggles as a woman with a disability—isolation, pain, and depression. "I can tell you," she confided, "because I know you get it." She was referring to my years of battling chronic illness and pain. Years that I've sometimes discarded as a waste, yet they were the very thing God used in that conversation. We talked about how sometimes people are reluctant to discuss another person's pain. It is too hard. Too uncomfortable.

My friend knew we shared the common bonds of suffering and grief. I was willing to enter her pain because it was familiar to me. Because God had comforted me in my troubles, I was able to comfort her. And because of her experiences, my friend offered me hope, compassion, and understanding as well.

Grief and suffering are still teachers I would rather not have. Their lessons come at a high cost. However, even though I entered that first tear-filled grief class full of fear and dread, I left the last class with a renewed sense of purpose. I would no longer avoid the pain of grief but instead embrace it as a new opportunity to share the love and comfort of Christ with others.

Dear God,

We praise You for being the Father of compassion. Thank You for not only comforting us in this life but also using us to provide comfort to others. Give us opportunities to show others Your compassion and caring. Amen.

Overcoming *Grief*

1. How has God comforted you in a time of grief?

2. What losses have you suffered that make you uniquely qualified to minister to someone? (Ex. loss of a spouse, a job, etc.)

3. Ask God to place you in the path of someone who needs comfort this week.

Chapter 5

Looking for Miracles

Is Anything Too Hard for Me?

Kristy

Jesus looked at them and said, "With man this is impossible, but with God all things are possible."
Matthew 19:26

Miracles come in many forms. Some are big. Others are seemingly small. Regardless, each miracle I've personally witnessed has pointed me to the Lord. The miracles have been so powerful that I know without a shadow of a doubt they were the handiwork of God.

I've experienced both big and small ones.

When I was a little girl, I had seizures. One day, I had a bad one. Mom knew I needed prompt medical attention and was driving me to the hospital when I quit breathing. She acted quickly and pulled into a market parking lot to seek help. This was obviously before cell phones existed. There happened to be a man at the market who got in the car and immediately began administering CPR while mom drove to the emergency room.

Once at the hospital, a doctor checked me over. Fortunately, I was alright after the seizure. The stranger from that store had helped save my life. When Mom went to look for the man to update and thank him, he was no longer there. She never had the opportunity to express her gratitude for his quick thinking and heroic act. He'd simply disappeared.

Over the years, Mom and I have talked about that day. I can't help but wonder if he was an angel in disguise. Did God send an angel that day? Maybe He did. Maybe not. Either way, I believe God placed him at the right place at the right time. Miracle.

Years later, pregnant with my own baby, my husband and I were told our child had a high probability of being born with several challenging medical issues including Robin Syndrome. If so, he would require immediate surgery to enable him to swallow. Medical staff suggested we should "consider our options" due to the severe health problems he would likely have. As far as we were concerned, it was a miracle I got pregnant in the first place considering my underlying health conditions. Our child wasn't an option.

We met with a pediatric surgeon, who arranged to be at the hospital at the time of delivery. My husband and I prayed throughout the pregnancy but rarely discussed our baby's possible health problems. We put our trust in God, hoping and praying for the best outcome. Whatever that looked like, whatever God's will, we were prepared to love our baby no matter what.

April rolled around, and with it, the time for our baby to be born. Moments before an emergency C-section, my doctor grabbed my hand and prayed. He didn't ask, he just prayed, fervently asking God for a smooth delivery and healthy baby. Zachary was born a few minutes later. He was perfect. He didn't have Robin Syndrome or any other physical health issues. No surgery required. Miracle.

As he grew, I learned that even small miracles count. As a young boy, Zac wanted to have his birthday party at a fun children's museum. We agreed, even though it was a bit pricey during a time when our budget was tight. We cut corners and trusted the Lord would provide the rest. We made a deposit at the museum, excited about the upcoming celebration. One day, out of the blue, a sweet neighbor came over and presented me with a greeting card. Lola explained she just wanted to give me a little gift as a thank you for being a good neighbor. It was so random. The card had money inside—the exact amount needed to pay the remainder for Zac's party. Miracle.

Those are just three examples of many more miracle stories I could share. To me, it's proof God provides and meets our needs. Sometimes He blesses us in ways we least expect.

"I am the LORD, the God of all mankind. Is anything too hard for me?" (Jeremiah 32:27).

Miracles are all around us. We must open our eyes to see them. Nothing is too hard for our miracle-making Father.

Dear Lord,

Thank You for the miracles You provide in my life. From the rising of the sun to its setting, You supply miraculous answers every day. Please strengthen my faith as I look toward You to see the big and small miracles You give me. Amen.

Growing in *Miracles*

1. How often do you take time to notice the miraculous in your life?

2. Think about the miracles you've witnessed. How has God surprised you?

3. In what ways has seeing miracles impacted you and your faith?

In Front of My Eyes

Sue

He is the one you praise; he is your God, who performed for you those great and awesome wonders you saw with your own eyes.

Deuteronomy 10:21

Our three girls were snuggled in the back seat of our old but reliable station wagon. We had just picked up my oldest daughter from a week-long Girl Scout camp. High-pitched giggles filled the car in between lines of a well-known camp song being sung in three-part unison, and all seemed well with the world. My husband and I looked at each other and smiled. Our little family was together once again.

The moment proved all too fragile. In a single instant their smiles were replaced with screams that filled the night air.

Two cars had been drag racing on the dark, two-lane country road we were traveling. As they came around the bend, the car in the lead hit us head on, 80 mph.

The next moments were filled with chaos and confusion. Wheels screeched, metal twisted, the girls whimpered. My husband, still, lay face down on the steering wheel. Broken glass surrounded me, and a painful burn radiated through my entire middle.

I pulled myself out of my mangled seat belt and managed to open the car door. Bright lights cut through the darkness. Not only had we been hit from the front, but we had also been hit from behind. Time seemed to freeze. I just stood there. Not knowing what to do next. A soft, gentle voice came out of nowhere.

"Sue, don't worry, I will help your husband and your girls."

I watched, as if viewing a movie scene. The man with black curly hair, rosy cheeks, and an Irish brogue lifted my husband from behind the wheel to the side of the road. He then proceeded to carry my daughters out of the car one by one and calmed them with his compassionate tone. Once he made sure we were all okay, he walked over to his black semi-truck parked across the road. We watched him hoist himself into the cab as the ambulance sirens got closer and closer.

Weeks later, as we entered a long season of healing, I called several places hoping to locate the man who removed us from our smoking, damaged vehicle. When I received a return call, I reiterated the description of the man and his truck to the person on the phone. Suddenly there was silence on the other end of the line.

"Ma'am, I was in the first ambulance that arrived at that scene. There was extreme wreckage on both sides of that winding road. A semi-truck could never have parked in the place you are describing. Also, I alerted both the police and witnesses with your request, and they stated, unequivocally, that there was no one fitting the description of the man you are describing anywhere near that accident."

A warm flush went through my body. I knew in an instant we had encountered an angel. One that had been sent to us in our moment of need. As I recalled his words, it hit me. He had used my name.

God provided a miracle for my family. In front of our very eyes. Apparently, for our eyes only. The five of us felt the kindness of his voice and his gentle, caring touch. No one else saw him. No one else heard him. It wasn't necessary. This miracle was for us alone.

Father,

Thank You for loving us enough to send angels our way. In the midst of trials, in the face of danger, You are there. I will sing of Your miracles all the days of my life. Amen.

Growing in *Miracles*

1. Can you recount a miracle of your own? What happened?

2. Do you believe miracles still happen today? Why or why not?

3. What are some ways you can let the world know of God's miracles?

God in Disguise

DeAnn

*But if I were you, I would appeal to God; I would
lay my cause before him. He performs wonders
that cannot be fathomed, miracles that cannot be
counted. Job 5:8-9*

I didn't realize it at the time, but grief sometimes disguises itself as
anger.

A few months after my father died, my mom drove from her
home in Mississippi to stay with my husband, our kids, and me in
Tennessee for a week. The absence of my dad was all-consuming.
Tempers flared, and I began to think our lives would never feel
peaceful or even remotely happy again.

One bad day, I prayed and asked God to intervene.

Lord, only you can fix this situation. Please help us love each other well. Give us assurance that we are going to survive this loss. Amen.

A desperate prayer for devastated hearts.

A few hours later, we decided to put aside our differences and go out for dinner. My mom wanted to eat at my dad's favorite Mexican restaurant. I wasn't sure it was a great idea, but the kids, my husband, and I all agreed to go. Just saying the words "party of five" instead of "party of six" to the hostess almost made me burst into tears.

After our food was served, our son, then age eleven, offered to pray. We typically pray as a family before a meal in a restaurant, but this time was different. Our daughter, then fifteen, must have sensed the tension because she specifically requested we all hold hands to pray. We did, and the mood shifted slightly for the better.

After the meal, our waitress came to present the check. She smiled and said, "You may find this hard to believe, but an older gentleman sitting on the other side of the room paid for all of your meals. He told me to tell you that he did this because he saw you holding hands and praying, and he rarely sees families praying together anymore."

We were stunned. I had witnessed my dad paying for meals for others, but no one had ever paid for a meal for any of us. I told our waitress that this man's gesture was so appreciated because my dad had died a few month's earlier and had loved this restaurant. I shared that this was our first meal there without him and how hard the day had been. The waitress started to cry.

We ran outside the restaurant to find the man to thank him and tell him his kindness came at an especially difficult time, but we never found him. I've often wondered if he was an angel or simply a human who listened to the urging of the Holy Spirit to meet our needs.

Grief may have tried to win that day by showing up as anger, but God unveiled His power and wonder in a miracle instead. Because sometimes, God's love mysteriously appears in a Mexican restaurant, camouflaged as an older gentleman with a generous heart.

Dear God,

We praise You for not only hearing our requests but responding to them in miraculous ways. Thank You for surprising us with miracles in the most unlikely places and for giving us glimpses of Your wonder and power here on earth. Amen.

Growing in *Miracles*

1. How has God revealed himself to you in a miracle? How has this strengthened your faith?

2. What miracles have surrounded you during an ordinary day?

3. How might God use you to be part of a miracle for someone else?

Chapter 6

Allowing Failure to

Teach

Epic Fails, Awesome God

Kristy

My flesh and my heart may fail, but God is the strength of my heart and my portion forever.
Psalm 73: 26

As a young girl, I tried most things without a second thought. Roller coasters. New jobs. Making new friends. The list could go on. When adulthood hit, I became more hesitant and fearful. I gradually developed a fear of heights, and roller coasters became out of the question. Just the thought of a new job brought on the fear of having a panic attack. As far as friendships, I became leery of those too because I'd been hurt. Today I have many friends, but my primary circle of friends, the ones who I trust to get close to, is relatively small. Somewhere along the way, I became guarded and fearful.

One of my biggest fears was the fear of failure. I didn't want to be a failure. I strived to accomplish something each day. If I didn't achieve what I set out to do, I felt as if the day was wasted, and I hated to feel like I was floundering. Today that fear of failure occasionally presents itself. If I'm not careful, it can consume me.

Failure covers a lot of ground. I think back to when I was a little girl. I loved to bake cupcakes with my Grandma Grace. We made them from scratch and prepared homemade icing using food coloring to make all different colors. They were so good.

However, my baking wasn't always successful.

Several years later, around age eleven, I decided to try baking mocha brownies on my own. I followed the recipe but used regular coffee instead of instant, which, as you can imagine, gave the whole batch a gritty texture. They were horrible. We threw them away—total kitchen fail. My brother still teases me about those brownies. Since then, I've had many kitchen disasters.

We all experience failures. I've certainly had my share. I have failed math tests, as that subject is not my strong suit. I have not always obeyed the speed limit, which landed me in driving school due to getting too many speeding tickets. I've fallen short of keeping my weight loss goals. Each time I've fallen, the Lord has allowed me to learn lessons that catapulted me forward.

We don't always come out unscathed from failures, but the good news is that we can rise and try again. It's important not to give up. You might be embarrassed due to a misstep. Well, guess what? You're not the only one. I've been embarrassed too. We all make mistakes in life. That's why pencils have erasers. We can't always erase our mistakes, but we can get up again to learn from them. You grow through what you go through and failing can be a learning experience. Perhaps the best lesson from failing is it brings us one step closer to being right the next time.

God goes before us and won't abandon us. Even with epic fails, we have an awesome God. He gives us hope for our future and can help us move forward. Beauty lies not in mistakes of the past but in the rising and perseverance that comes from His help. Pick yourself up, dust yourself off, and seek the heavenly Father.

Do not let failures define you. Instead, let them refine you, and pray for the Lord to redeem you. No matter how far you have fallen or how badly you have failed, you can still overcome with strength from the Lord. If you're dwelling on your past mistakes, don't stay discouraged. Don't dwell on who you are because of failures. Instead, remember Whose you are in spite of them. You are His. You're a loved child of God. Lift your head. Seek His face. Move forward by the strength He gives.

Dear Lord,

Thank You for loving me despite my failures. Help me remember I am not defined by them, but I am refined and redeemed by You. Amen.

Overcoming *Failure*

1. Name a failure that has set you back.

2. How were you able to move forward with the Lord's help?

3. What have you learned from these struggles?

The Unraveling Thread

Sue

And call on me in the day of trouble; I will deliver you, and you will honor me. Psalm 50:15

Curled up in a fetal position on my bed, I cried, "How did I get here, Lord?" My marriage of twenty-five years was finished. I had just signed my home over to my ex-husband. Due to some very poor, emotion-led decisions, my business was failing. And on top of it all, I found myself homeless. Once again, I had no choice but to start over.

Starting over—a familiar phrase throughout my life. Repositioning. Recreating. Renewing. Revisiting. From a very young age,

I had walked a road less traveled, scattered with rumble strips. Less traveled because no one wanted to go there. Taking one step forward and hitting those bumps slowed me down every time. My attitude struggled to maintain its positive edge. Those who knew me well recognized that backing down from a challenge was not in my wheelhouse. But this time was different. I didn't want to admit it. Failure had knocked on my door, and I let her in.

From the moment the Lord entered my life, I watched Him perform miracle after miracle around me and in me. Walking through harrowing experiences and carrying me out of proverbial burning buildings. I wasn't sure about this time, though. The thread was unraveling in front of me at an alarming pace. All I could hear was a mantra in my head—*You are a failure with a capital F.*

As soon as those words had been spoken aloud in my mind, I was reminded of another sad time in my life. Someone asked if there was anything in my life that God had not brought me through. Hmmm. I took a long pause before answering. My mind circled around the multitude of events in my life journey. I couldn't name a thing. It was apparent to myself and everyone who knew me, God had taken me through to the other side of all the bad and ugly. Yes, I bore scars, some still very fresh, but they were healing. My heart was beating to tell about it.

Failure sure has some irritating bedfellows, doesn't she? There is shame and anxiety. Their friends, depression, fear, and pain, are always close behind. And who can forget their leechy cousins, self-loathing and resentment?

Walking on all those hot coals, I suddenly felt the Lord pick me up, put salve on my feet, and hold me tenderly while long-suffering tears slid down my face. A pastor from back home who knew what I was going through sent me a letter: "Sue, God wants you to know that He sees over your big wall. He is taller than you. He knows what is on the other side. Just hold His hand. Trust him. Believe in Him. More than anything, allow Him to walk with you through this next season. You will get through this. Look for Him. His hand is reaching out for yours." I've never forgotten those words. They were words of hope, of a future on the other side of failure.

That night, I crawled off that bed, wiped my tears, and got on my knees. God had opened a portal for me to call upon Him once again. I humbly asked for forgiveness. Spent a long time being honest. Placed my failures at His feet and looked up.

I am not a failure because I am a daughter of the Most High King. God didn't throw me away like a piece of spoiled garbage. Instead, He loved me more.

Now, as I look back through the years to that time, I don't see failure. In its place, I see promises shining brightly from God. Promises that He will never leave me, never forsake me, and will love me forever.

Dear Lord,

Thank You for loving me well. You replaced my failures with Your promises. I will exalt You for all my breaths. Amen.

Overcoming *Failure*

1. Has failure ever knocked at your door? How did you respond to her request?

2. Can you name one thing that God has not brought you through?

3. What did God remind you of when you felt like a failure?

The Hidden Side
of Failure

DeAnn

But he said to me, "My grace is sufficient for you, for my power is made perfect in weakness." Therefore I will boast all the more gladly about my weaknesses, so that Christ's power may rest on me. That is why, for Christ's sake, I delight in weaknesses, in insults, in hardships, in persecutions, in difficulties. For when I am weak, then I am strong. 2 Corinthians 12:9-10

I read the following words, or similar versions, almost daily on the parent Facebook page from the company where my daughter interned.

"My child is so upset and disappointed that her internship at Disney World was cancelled. All she has done for the past month is sit in her room and cry. She even refuses to unpack. She can't seem to accept the fact that she won't be going back."

Granted, these were disappointing times. Our daughter, age twenty, had taken a semester break from college to start her dream internship at Disney World in January of 2020—only to be hit with the hard news in March that the park was closing for an unforeseeable amount of time due to Covid-19. All interns were called into a room on a Friday and told that their last day of work would be the following Sunday. Both parents and students were in shock.

Our son, a sophomore in high school, had been told school would be closed for at least a month, probably longer. We packed up his locker, wondering when he would be able to enter the familiar halls and see his friends again.

After a whirlwind family trip to Orlando to pack our daughter's apartment and bring her home, we tried our best as a family to settle into this "new normal." There were a few tears shed, but, overall, there was surprisingly little drama or disappointment from either of the kids. They found some classes they were interested in online, organized group video chats with their friends, set new bedtimes of 3:00 a.m., and ate about $500 of groceries per day.

About a month into this new life, I kept reading more posts on the Facebook page about other kids weeping in their rooms because of their disappointment, and I thought that maybe our kids were just trying to hide their true feelings. So I asked them, "Are you two really okay? I know this is a hard time, and it is normal to feel sad or upset because of such drastic changes."

And you know what they said? "Mom, we are good. Really. It's kind of nice to have a break and relax."

I thought back to the times I had asked—no, honestly, begged —God to fill in the gaps of my parenting with His grace. Not that I thought I was such a terrible parent, but I definitely had limits. Pretty drastic ones at times.

Since I had struggled with a chronic illness and pain their entire lives, there were many, many days that the best I could do was make sure my kids were fed and not allowed near sharp objects. I spent so many days lying on the couch with the television blaring *Barney* or *Sesame Street* songs that I was convinced my kids would think normal moms never sat upright and only wore pajamas all day.

Even to this day, our vacation schedule goes something like "Let's plan to leave on Tuesday, but hope we are at least packed and in the car by Thursday." No one knows when or where or what will happen. It's a total gamble depending on how much pain I have on which day. I once told my husband that our only hope for our kids was to save enough money to pay for the counseling they would need as adults because of all I could not do during their childhood.

But then.

As I sat, worrying that the kids were really falling apart inside and afraid to share their feelings, I read 2 Corinthians 12:9. "My grace is sufficient for you, for my power is made perfect in weakness." It was as if God audibly said to me, "I am filling in the gaps with My grace, just like you asked. Maybe the reason your kids are resilient and can handle adversity is because I am using your biggest weakness for My glory. Maybe the uncertainties and lack of predictability in your life are just what I needed to prepare your kids to do My work."

Well, how about that.

Imagine being loved so much by God that He is willing to fill in the gaps, no matter how deep or wide. Even when I feel like a failure, I can throw off the weight of guilt and look at my weaknesses and say, "What potential." or "Wonder how God is going to use this?" For when I am weak, He will show up. Just as He promised.

Dear Jesus,

Thank You for my weaknesses. Help me see them as opportunities instead of failures and as chances for others to see Your power. Please continue to fill in my gaps with Your grace and help me realize that Your grace is enough. Amen.

Overcoming *Failure*

1. What weaknesses have you tried to hide from others?

2. How can God turn your weaknesses into strengths for His plan?

3. How can you encourage others who feel defeated?

Chapter 7

Persevering When We Want to Quit

Mind Renewal

Kristy

*Look to the LORD and his strength; seek his face
always. 1 Chronicles 16:11*

If you are like me, your mind occasionally runs away with negative thoughts. I sometimes imagine every bad outcome before a problem has even begun. Recently, I had an issue with my left breast. I'd had a mammogram a few months prior with normal results. However, since I'd been having odd symptoms, the nurse practitioner at a breast clinic wanted me to have an ultrasound to be on the safe side.

The procedure was scheduled on a dreary, rainy afternoon. Traffic was awful. Then it took a long time to find a place to park in the crowded lot. Already stressed, I went inside to get checked in and sat down in the waiting area. I looked around and saw others dealing with the side effects of chemo and various therapies. My stress level increased. I was afraid, and my mind began to wander. *Do I have breast cancer?* My thoughts kept spinning, thinking over all the worst-case scenarios.

After my name was called, the kind technician quickly put me at ease. Once she was finished with the ultrasound, she said, "I need to go talk to the radiologist, and I'll be right back." No sooner had she left the room than my mind went back to thinking the worst. I just knew it would be bad news. Cancer. I was sure of it. I thought, *Oh my gosh. I don't have time for this.* I had a writing deadline coming up in a few months. *The treatments will make me so sick, and I won't be able to write.* My mind ran off the rails.

The tech returned to the room and said, "The radiologist compared today's results to your latest mammogram, and everything looks good. All clear. Just follow up with your doctor if you have any other problems."

Whew. I let out a big sigh of relief. No chemo needed. No cancer. My mind had already convinced me I was sick and basically dying.

Our minds are so powerful, but they can tell us lies. I believe those lies are straight from the enemy, and we often believe them. We fall for them hook, line, and sinker. Often, we build up and suffer through problems in our minds before we ever encounter an actual problem. As my husband says, "We borrow trouble."

My dad often told me, "You can do anything you set your mind to." He taught me about perseverance. It's true I have been able to set my mind to achieving goals. I've worked hard to accomplish tasks and have knuckled down with determination. Yet when it comes to persevering with my thoughts, that's another story. My mind seems to forget God is already in the future, and I start "borrowing trouble." I worry and freak out about what might happen rather than allow God to guide my thoughts and bring me peace.

Romans 8:6 reads, "The mind governed by the flesh is death, but the mind governed by the Spirit is life and peace."

Left to my own devices, I'm doomed. Thankfully the Lord has mercy on us and shows us much needed compassion. If I keep persevering with my thoughts focused on God and allow my mind to be led by the Spirit as in Romans 8:6, I will have that peace.

To engage in the process of renewing our minds, we must trust God. Trusting Him will help us. With the Lord's help, we can move forward through life's trials. Instead of thinking negative thoughts, seek the Lord and His strength. Let's persevere with peaceful thoughts, knowing He's there for us even if something bad does happen. Instead of becoming undone, let's look to our heavenly Father and entrust our thoughts to Him for a mind renewal.

Dear Lord,

When I go into worry mode and borrow trouble, thank You for being there to help redirect my thoughts. I praise You for bringing me peace. Even when problems do arise, please help renew my mind so that I may focus on You to persevere through whatever comes my way. Amen.

Growing in *Perseverance*

1. Does your mind run away and automatically go to worrisome, troubling thoughts? If so, how can you stop it?

2. Do you easily seek the Lord to renew your mind, or is that difficult for you to do? Why?

3. How different would your life be if you focused on the Lord and allowed Him to lead your thoughts? Would you then persevere in peace rather than focus on the negative?

Persevering through the Smallest Miracle

Sue

For you created my inmost being; you knit me together in my mother's womb. I praise you because I am fearfully and wonderfully made; your works are wonderful, I know that full well.

Psalm 139:13-14

Have you had that baby yet?" As I was nearly two weeks overdue, this question played like a broken record.

My second pregnancy was far from being a textbook case. In my third month, I began having complications. I had prayed for this little one. I had welcomed the nausea, the headaches, and the other "normal for me" experiences that occurred as my body prepared a cozy, albeit temporary, home for my child to grow in before entering this world.

As new issues arose, my doctor ordered bed rest. Those words alone were hard for my personality but having a 2-year-old running around made it even more difficult. But I knew, though, I needed to carry on. As I felt my child growing within my belly, I began to pray in a different way. "Lord, I need Your strength to do this. Your strength to keep me still. Your strength to help me persevere."

So there I lay, day after day, getting up only to use the bathroom. I ate on that couch, read stories, rocked my toddler to sleep, and prayed. Even though I did everything required of me, the doctor called to give some disturbing news. They found spots on my baby's kidneys. Further tests would need to be performed once the infant was born. They talked about dialysis and ongoing care.

I felt numb at first. After all, everyone hopes and prays for a healthy, bouncing baby. Once it all settled in, though, the numbness dissipated, and my faith kicked in. Everyone around me wore a sad face. They meant well, they truly did. This was a shock to all of us. We were such young parents. But I don't do well with sadness, never have. Sad wasn't going to help me or this little one. I was in for the long haul. My feet were planted to persevere.

I sent my sister to the library, read as much as I could on the subject, and prayed for my positive attitude to kick into high gear. We could do this. No matter what challenges came our way. We asked our church to pray, and we waited.

Sarah Marie was born in a whirlwind of flurry. Right after I held my sweet daughter, they whisked her off for those aforementioned tests. Her daddy and I waited in strained anticipation. Then suddenly, they brought our sweet daughter in with a warming bed and told us the doctor would be in soon.

As my baby suckled on her knuckle, I felt a giggle rise inside of me. This feisty little girl was the healthiest little baby I had ever seen. She had cooked in my womb for almost 10 months. Her chunky little fingers and toes wiggled energetically. It was hard to believe that there was anything wrong.

The doctor knocked on the door and got right down to business. With tears in his eyes, he looked at us and said, "I don't say this often, but your little girl is a miracle. I was sure this conversation was going to go another way. But the tests all show that her kidneys are completely clear."

Our very own miracle. Right in front of our eyes.

We were prepared to take care of our daughter in whatever way was needed. No matter what the news might have been. That fact that stood loud in our hearts. I don't know why God chose to perform a miracle on our daughter, but He did. He had a specific plan for her life. One that didn't include problems with her kidneys. I promised that very day to raise this child in the love and the fear of the Lord.

She has walked in her faith, and it shines all over her life. Our smallest miracle has grown into a young woman who has shared the gospel of Jesus Christ with thousands of people around the world. Her smile is wide and true. Her life has touched many.

God had a plan. A plan that involved persevering. Had I decided to sit back and give up, the entire experience would have read differently. I've grown to know that He loves my daughter so much more than I ever could. This plan was not just for me, but I'm so glad He picked me to share it with.

> *Dear Lord,*
>
> *I can't imagine going through life without You. More than anything, thank You for helping us persevere and for shining Your plans so brightly in this dark world. Amen.*

Growing in *Perseverance*

1. Can you see the grand plan God has for your life and how He has helped you persevere? Explain.

2. How were you able to keep going during a stressful time?

3. What have you learned when you persevered?

Not Your Typical

Perseverance

DeAnn

Therefore, since we are surrounded by such a great cloud of witnesses, let us throw off everything that hinders and the sin that so easily entangles. And let us run with perseverance the race marked out for us, fixing our eyes on Jesus, the pioneer and perfecter of our faith. For the joy set before him he endured the cross, scorning its shame, and sat down at the right hand of the throne of God. Consider him who endured such opposition from sinful men, so that you will not grow weary and lose heart. Hebrews 12:1-3

My whole life, I have wanted to achieve a label of three words: Results Not Typical.

Many late nights, I got sucked into the world of infomercials, and sometimes even ordered what they were selling—cooking utensils, self-help programs promising I could walk across hot coals, miracle makeup, weight loss pills—you name it. The only problem was a tiny disclaimer at the bottom of the screen stating that perhaps this particular program might not work for everyone. You've seen it: *Results Not Typical. Yet I always thought I could be one of the few, the proud, the thin, and the beautiful who persevered and completed the program.

Several years and many "low, low credit card payments" later, I realized a hard truth. I was typical. I was not a chef. Even with my new tools, I could not make a watermelon basket or fruit balls. My makeup would never look flawless, even with the magic minerals. I would never make the vegetable drinks with the juicer and lose thirty pounds. I could not walk across a hot sidewalk, much less flaming coals. Typical.

Fast forward a few years, and I was playing putt-putt golf with my husband and son. Suddenly, I struggled to pick up my ball. Not because of arthritis, but because of a very thick stomach. Not being able to bend over became the final straw. I joined a weight loss program and encouraged my husband to join too.

I was convinced this was just another futile attempt to better myself. I even told the teacher, "Look, we are terrible at these programs. We paid for a month, but don't expect us to come back after about week two." She laughed like she couldn't tell if I was serious or not. I was.

But something strange happened. We started losing weight. We decided we could do the program a week at a time.

Our weight loss journey became a spiritual journey as well. Every time I felt weak and tempted, I prayed. I thought of Jesus. The hardest struggle was nighttime snacking. My husband actually suggested we take over-the-counter sleep aids and go to bed at 6:00 p.m. to avoid raiding the pantry. But I told myself that if Jesus endured the pain of the cross for me, surely I could deal with a few hunger pangs. I wanted to be a healthier person to serve Him better. I wanted to live longer to raise my children to follow Him.

We started "running the race marked out for us" as described in Hebrews 12:1. Every day felt like a marathon. We were hungry, but we kept going, surrounded by people in our weight loss group who encouraged us and cheered us on. My Bible version (NIV) says that the "cloud of witnesses" who surround us daily are not spectators but inspiring examples. We had many. Some members had even lost one hundred pounds.

Hebrews 12 also tells us to throw off anything that hinders us, and we did this. I almost cried the day I threw a pie in the garbage so I wouldn't eat it. But it worked. No pie, no temptation.

Four months later, I walked to the front of the class to accept my award for losing twenty-five pounds. My husband lost forty. We both became lifetime members. And most importantly, we were *Results Not Typical. We had done it, finally!

Imagine our disappointment when, a year later, after months spent at home during a pandemic, my husband and I had both gained back ten pounds each. We felt discouraged. My immediate thoughts said maybe we were typical after all. We both felt too tired to start the weight loss journey again.

But isn't weight loss a lot like life in general? One month we are successful, reaching new goals, and the next we are struggling, wondering if we can even make it five more minutes without a piece of chocolate cake. We finally get the house organized one week and then sit in piles of papers and laundry the next. It seems like a constant battle just to survive, much less be "results not typical."

What I didn't realize years ago was, as a Christian, I was never typical. When I gave my life to Christ, I became a new creation, with the power of the Holy Spirit living in me. He gives me strength and helps me persevere when I want to give up. He will help me restart the diet, work the extra hours, finish the impossible class, save the needed money, or believe in the wayward child. He renews me when my own willpower is gone.

You may not need to lose weight, but you can apply these truths from the Bible to whatever challenges you are facing. Run whatever race you are in, one day at a time. Throw off everything which trips you up—negative thoughts, chocolate, or other people's opinions. Focus on Christ and remember how He suffered and persevered. Look to others for encouragement and try to provide it to them as well. And remember, you don't have to walk to the front of a classroom and receive a prize to know you are not typical. With the power of Christ in your life, you will be the exception.

Dear Jesus,

We praise You for Your example of perseverance. Show us the race You have marked out for us and give us strength to finish well. Help us to encourage others in their races too. Amen.

Growing in *Perseverance*

1. What particular race are you in?

2. What do you need to set aside in order to run your race?

3. How can you encourage others to persevere? How can you show others they are not typical?

Chapter 8

Forgiving with No Strings Attached

Redemption & Grace

Kristy

In him we have redemption through his blood, the forgiveness of sins, in accordance with the riches of God's grace. Ephesians 1:7

As a young student, I walked into my classroom early one morning to find a snake on the floor directly in front of my desk. I quickly told my teacher. She crossed her arms, rolled her eyes, and stayed where she was. In a louder tone, I said, "Really, there's a snake in front of my desk!" She walked over, and guess what? There was a snake in front of my desk.

The teacher jumped on my desk chair and screamed. It was hilarious and frightening at the same time. I'm terrified of snakes. I don't remember what happened to the snake, but I've never forgotten the incident. My teacher later explained she thought one of my classmates had thrown a rubber snake in front of my desk as a joke. It was not a joke. That snake was alive.

I could've been upset with my teacher for not believing me, but I didn't harbor any resentment. I understood where she was coming from because we did, indeed, have a class full of characters. I can see how she thought someone had placed a toy snake there to play a prank.

Admittedly, there have been other times in my life when I haven't been as forgiving. I've been bitter and had an unforgiving heart. Carrying around unforgiveness is heavy. Little by little, it eats away at you—slowly gnawing at your conscience. It's like a snake slithering in and causing chaos.

I'm typically good at forgiving others. It's the whole "forgiving myself" part that tends to cause me the most trouble. I remember a time I was so terribly burdened by something I'd done, ashamed and drowning in guilt.

One Sunday, our pastor at the time offered a few moments during the service for anyone who wanted to go to the altar and pray. He made himself available for those who wanted someone to pray with them. One sin of mine weighed especially heavy on me. So I went up and spilled the beans to the pastor. I told him I knew the Lord had forgiven me. I just could not forgive myself.

He looked me square in the eyes and said, "Kristy, would you ever give a small child a basket full of bricks too heavy for him to carry?"

I replied with a confident, "No."

He looked at me with a comforting smile and said, "God wants you to put down the basket." He then prayed with me, and I suddenly felt the weight of guilt and shame lighten. I learned to put down the basket.

That, my friends, is the beauty of forgiveness.

I often remember the "basket full of bricks" story. When God forgives us, He doesn't expect us to keep carrying around the heavy load of guilt and shame. When God forgives, He doesn't hold onto it. Neither should we.

If you need to forgive someone, I encourage you to do it. It doesn't always come easy, but having an unforgiving spirit is heavy. You are weighing yourself down unnecessarily—even if you're having a difficult time forgiving yourself.

Jesus died on the cross for our sins. Let's not forget that. He's already paid the price for a debt we no longer owe and cannot repay. We only need to sincerely repent of our sins, and the Lord forgives us without condemnation or question. He wipes the slate clean. Why don't you give yourself the same courtesy? Redemption and grace are beautiful.

Dear Jesus,

Thank You for dying on the cross for my sins and for the gift of forgiveness. Please help me to forgive others as well as myself. Remind me to put down the heavy load You don't want me to carry. I love You Lord. Amen.

Growing in *Forgiveness*

1. Is it hard for you to forgive others? What about forgiving yourself?

2. Examine your heart for unforgiveness. What do you see?

3. How do you feel when you receive forgiveness as well as when you forgive others?

Quick to Forgive

Sue

And forgive us our trespasses, as we forgive them
that trespass against us. Matthew 6:12 (NMB)

Forgiveness has many facets. It's what I would call a "complicated" action. You would be hard pressed to find anyone who would truthfully say it's their first reaction when facing a difficult situation. As humans, we tend to "sit in our stuff" first and allow it to swirl around us like a tornado in a deadly storm. Anger. Bitterness. Hate. Jealousy. Contempt. Rage. Believe it or not, these feelings are easy to embrace. But forgiveness, well, that is a much harder process.

Imagine a world that obtains a posture of quick-to-forgive and slow-to-anger, instead of the other way around. How different would the world look? Would it take on an entirely different shade? Unfortunately, most times, this isn't our first response. Instead, we process like a video game with multiple levels. We jump through hoops. Trying to avoid new dangers. Weave in and out to dodge moving targets. Then, more often than not, we find ourselves in the fail zone. Not leveling up. Having to start all over from the beginning.

Wouldn't the opposite be so much simpler? Take less time? And more than anything, help us avoid wounds along the way?

A new life recipe needs to be created for forgiveness to arise in our land. One sprinkled with a healthy dose of amazing grace. Jesus showed us forgiveness is an essential ingredient.

"Forgive us our trespasses, as we forgive them who trespass against us." The word trespass means we have gone somewhere we were not invited to go, committing an offense against the person or his property. Forgive us our sins, as we forgive them who sinned against us. It's clear cut. We have sinned. Others have sinned. We have sinned against others. Others have sinned against us. Conflict resolution: forgive.

God was specific. He knew how to forgive because He was familiar with it. He forgave us.

In an episode of *Little House on the Prairie,* young Laura thought God wouldn't talk to her because of all the bad she had done. Jonathan, a proposed angel in the mountains, said, "No child, He is forgiving. He has to be, or else He wouldn't have anyone else to talk to.[1]" That took my breath away. God doesn't just forgive some. He doesn't pick and choose. There are no lists. He doesn't throw dice to see who wins His affection and quality time. When we ask

---

1   Little House on the Prairie. 1974. "The Lord Is My Shepherd (Part 2)," NBC, December 18.

for forgiveness, He just does it. He loves us. It's not His desire that we continue to sit in our sin alone. He desires to talk and commune with us.

What's even more astonishing is that once He forgives, He forgets. Picture writing your sin on a blackboard. You show it to the Lord. You humbly ask for forgiveness. God reaches down into a bucket of water with a sponge in it. He wrings out the sponge and thoroughly wipes the sin away. No memory of it is left. The blackboard is erased. The sin is gone.

Here's to a world that gets an update. A world filled with forgiveness. Shines with a new hue. Painted with a fresh coat of the paint of forgiveness.

Dear Lord,

Forgive us for not forgiving quickly. Help us to be more like You. Give us a different lens through which we can see Your children like You see them. Provide us with the means to forgive and forget their trespasses against us. Help us, Father, to walk in Your footsteps of forgiveness. More than anything, thank You for forgiving us completely, thoroughly, and unconditionally. Amen.

Growing in *Forgiveness*

1. What road do you travel upon when driving to forgiveness? The one that holds onto the memory or the one that wipes a slate clean? Why?

2. When you forgive, is it conditional? Explain.

3. Is there someone in your life right now who you need to forgive? How can you take steps toward forgiveness?

Learning Forgiveness

DeAnn

The LORD is compassionate and gracious, slow to anger, abounding in love. He will not always accuse, nor will he harbor his anger forever; he does not treat us as our sins deserve or repay us according to our iniquities. For as high as the heavens are above the earth, so great is his love for those who fear him; as far as the east is from the west, so far has he removed our transgressions from us. Psalm 103:8-12

As a small child, I loved playing board games. The trouble came when I lost a game with neighborhood friends. Soon afterwards, a friend or two would disappear from our home.

My mother would come into the room and say, "Where is your friend?"

"I had to send her home," I would reply.

"Why?" she would ask, bewildered.

"Because she won the game, and I was supposed to win. That's unfair."

I would stomp my feet and march off, crying.

My poor mom. She had a hard road with me. I can't tell you how many times she had to make me apologize and invite the banished guest back to our house. Over and over, my mom tried to explain to me how the other person might feel—how she might want to win too and feel hurt about being sent home. My four-year-old self was not the least bit interested in learning empathy. I wanted to win.

Learning to ask for forgiveness did not come easy to me. Pride was a big obstacle to overcome, even then. I would pout for a while, dwell on how I had been wronged, and try to play by myself. After getting bored with my own company, I would shuffle across the street, hang my head, and mumble something to the evicted guest about being sorry. In my mind, forgiveness consisted of the friend agreeing to come back and play, nothing more.

Many years later, friendships and marriage taught me another side of forgiveness—extending forgiveness. When my friend or spouse truly wronged me and then asked for forgiveness, I still wanted to resort to my childlike feelings. *You have no idea how badly you hurt me. I didn't deserve this. You need to pay for hurting me.* The thoughts replayed over and over in my mind.

Not only did I repeat the thoughts, I rarely missed an opportunity to remind the offender how he or she had hurt me in the past. Yes, even after I had allegedly forgiven the person. I could whisper forgiveness one week and drag the offense back out a year later in another disagreement.

Today, when I read the Bible, I am so thankful God's ways are not like mine. Psalm 103 reminds me the Lord is compassionate and gracious, slow to anger, abounding in love. He doesn't treat us as we deserve or repay us for our sins. He doesn't send us away as punishment. He never reminds us of our mistakes; in fact, He has removed our sins as far away as the east is from the west.

So much of our society today has a "send them home" mentality. Anyone who has a different opinion on social media is immediately unfriended or blocked. Empathy is nowhere to be found. Forgiveness is lacking. Any perceived offense is replayed over and over. Some might offer a weak apology from time to time to appease or manipulate; but true repentance is absent, much as it was in my childhood self. Yet, in Ephesians 4:31-32, Paul reminds us to "Get rid of all bitterness, rage, and anger, brawling and slander, along with every form of malice. Be kind and compassionate to one another, forgiving each other, just as in Christ God forgave you."

There's the key: "just as in Christ God forgave you." When we realize how much God loves us and has forgiven us by sending His Son to die for us, we can't help but be filled with compassion and forgiveness for others.

Many days, my childish self tries to re-emerge. I have to work at forgiveness. I still like to win. But I've won the gift of God's forgiveness, and there's no better prize than that.

Dear God,

Thank You for the incredible gift of Your forgiveness. I am forever grateful that You not only forgive but forget my wrongdoings. Let me become slow to anger and quick to forgive. Bless my relationships and help me model Your forgiveness to others. Amen.

Growing in *Forgiveness*

1. How could your life be different if you decided to forgive like God?

2. Do you bring up hurtful events from the past to the offender? If so, how can you stop?

3. When has "winning" been more important to you than apologizing and saving a relationship?

Chapter 9

Building Strength in Moments of Weakness

It's About Time

Kristy

God is our refuge and strength, an ever-present help in trouble. Psalm 46:1

My husband had an opportunity for a promotion with his company. We lived in East Tennessee at the time, and his interview was in Georgia. He wanted me to accompany him on the trip, and I wanted to go for moral support but didn't think I could find the strength. I had battled debilitating depression on and off for a few years. At that time, I had spiraled down so far I could barely put one foot in front of the other—let alone go on a trip. That would have required more energy than I could muster. I could barely get out of bed. To say the depression was bad would be an understatement.

I was diagnosed with bipolar disorder less than a year after I'd graduated from college. Prior to my diagnosis, I would laugh one minute, cry the next, and exhibit other out-of-character behaviors. This led to my first admission to a psychiatric hospital. That turned out to be the first of many hospitalizations for the depression, anxiety, and suicidal ideations stemming from bipolar. Fortunately, I never attempted suicide, but I sure did think about it at times. I'd get so low that I felt helpless, hopeless, useless, and worthless. At one point, I even planned my own funeral.

There I was, several years after the initial diagnosis, and I found myself sitting at the top of our stairs—crying about the trip. In desperation, I started praying and pleading with the Lord. For the first time in my life, I was mad at God. I said, "Lord, you've promised you'll never leave me or forsake me. If you're not going to help me, I'm just going to pull myself up by the bootstraps and get on with my life." I thought about this for a moment. Of course I knew standing on my own strength wouldn't work. Then I said, "Okay Lord, I need you." In a still small voice, I heard God say, "It's about time." I knew in an instant that He'd heard my cry and He was with me.

He gives us strength to keep moving forward. When we're deep in the pit of darkness, He is our light. He is our refuge, our strength, and our help in times of trouble.

I gradually started feeling better and was able to go on the trip. My husband got the promotion. We moved to Georgia, and I'm thankful for our time living there. Two years later, with yet another promotion, we moved back to Tennessee, but I hold our time in Georgia and the sweet friendships I made there very dear. God renewed my faith and strengthened my mind, body, and spirit during that season.

I still occasionally struggle with bouts of depression and anxiety, but I'm grateful to be doing well now. The good news is that Jesus always hears our cries and pulls us through our trials. He gives us strength to carry on through His power, even at our weakest. I believe He specializes in strengthening us at our weakest. Just remember there's help and hope in the name of the Lord.

Dear Lord,

Thank You for hearing my cries and for loving me enough to pull me out of the pit. When I'm stuck in the mud and mire of darkness, I'm grateful it's You who lifts me up. Thanks for being my light, my refuge, and my strength. When I face trouble, thanks for helping me. Amen.

Growing in *Strength*

1. Have you ever been angry with God? If so, how did you get past it?

2. Think of a specific time when you called out to God for help. How did He answer your prayers?

3. How did the Lord provide you with strength during a time of trouble?

Running to the Strong Tower

Sue

The name of the LORD is a strong tower; the
righteous man runs into it and is safe.
Proverbs 18:10 (ESV)

A storm was coming. I could feel it. From a young age, my body has alerted me to changes in weather patterns. I get pressure headaches. They throw me off kilter. Make me feel ungrounded, disconnected. My husband calls me a human barometer. These changes let me know a storm is brewing on the horizon.

The first week we moved to Tennessee, the sky looked ominous when suddenly, blaring alarms resounded in the streets. I looked at my girls, fear in my throat, and grabbed some blankets before proceeding to stuff everyone, including the dog, into the closet underneath the stairs. We didn't have a basement.

We had been warned throughout the day about the possibility of tornadoes. This was a new experience for us Northerners. Thunderstorms? They come and they go. We've been through hundreds of them. Snow? No problem, just switch the SUV to four wheel drive. Ice and hail? Just downshift and follow the salt truck.

This was different. The thought of a huge, swirling cone of wind emitting enough power to lift a house off its foundation made the hair on my arms stand at attention and turned my stomach queasy. After all, I had seen those movies where the destruction was massive and immediate. My mind started concocting all kinds of images.

I realized it wasn't so much the storm that was freaking me out, it was the feeling of being powerless. My resolve to control what was looming above us had dissipated into a fearful weakness. As we sat huddled together, listening to the winds pick up, my heart made me feel very human. It was bouncing around inside my chest like a tornado all its own. I looked around from face to face. Everyone I cared deeply about was in this closet with me. I began to pray. I prayed for the strength of God to fill that little space. We didn't need a basement. We already had access to a strong tower. All we had to do was run into it.

Since that day, we have experienced dozens of tornadoes. I still have my little space in the closet. That is just wisdom on my part. But I no longer fear what can happen, I trust that whatever does happen, I can rely on God's strength to pull me through.

That little closet has turned into my "tornado prayer closet." It has transformed into a place of comfort. My heavenly Father and I have some great conversations when the storms loom large. This space reminds me that I need to run, not hide, into His strong tower.

Father,

You knew I would need a strong tower. A place where I could go and meet You for security and stability. My fear evaporates when I am with You. Thank You for Your unlimited and unconditional strength. Your loving arms give me the strength I need to deal with the storms in my life. Amen.

Growing in *Strength*

1. Where do you go when storms become overwhelming in your life? What would it look like to run into God's strong tower as soon as the winds of life begin to pick up?

2. People watch us closely as we react to situations. What do others see when storms surround you?

3. God knew we would need His strength. How often do you rely on your own strength rather than His? What are some reminders from His Word you can cling to when you're tempted to doubt or forget His power?

Developing Strength

DeAnn

Let us not become weary in doing good, for at the proper time we will reap a harvest if we do not give up. Galatians 6:9

I was athletically challenged in middle school. In fact, I was fired from Physical Education class. Yes, you read that right. Terminated from PE.

How was that possible for a tiny, five-foot-two-inch girl, weighing in at ninety-five pounds? I was in a class of super athletic girls who were much bigger than I was. We happened to be playing volleyball, and I was terrified of getting hit by a ball. Not a good combination.

Not only was I afraid of the ball, but I also could not serve it over the net to save my life. Every time I had to serve, I would make a fist and pound the ball as hard as my skinny arm could. If I was lucky, it would travel five feet. Not even close to going over the net. Once I even managed to serve the ball behind me. The other girls, none too amused, would yell at me after each pitiful attempt.

I guess my PE teacher took notice, because a few weeks later, I was called into the principal's office. The principal said he had a need for someone to pick up attendance slips every morning, so he offered to give me a PE credit if I would work in the office instead of going to the gym. He made me feel like I would be doing him a favor. I accepted within two seconds and had to refrain from jumping across the desk and hugging him with all my might.

Fast forward thirty years, and I am setting up a volleyball net with my two kids, ages 13 and 9. The memories came flooding back.

"Kids, you won't believe this, but your mom was so terrible at sports that I was once kicked out of PE class."

"Mom, nobody gets kicked out of PE."

"Well, I did." I went on to tell them the details of my short-lived volleyball career. "Just watch," I said confidently, as I started my first attempt at serving the ball.

What happened next was nothing short of a miracle. Not only did the ball sail over the net, it went all the way into the neighbor's yard.

"Mom. You said you couldn't serve. But look." The kids jumped up and down with excitement.

"That was just a fluke," I responded. "Let me try again."

And there it went. Another ball flying over the net with a height I had never seen.

"You did it, Mom. You're a volleyball champ."

After serving about twenty more balls successfully, I started trying to figure out what had happened over the years. How did I gain so much strength?

And then I realized that for the past thirteen years, I had basically been training with weights. Two to be exact. I rocked babies daily, lifted gazillion-pound car seats, manipulated strollers the size of a small car, and balanced babies while successfully maneuvering a shopping cart filled to the brim.

Paul tells us in Galatians 6:9 to not become weary in doing good because we will eventually reap a harvest if we don't give up. I didn't know that every time I was lifting, serving, pushing, and pulling my kids, I was developing strength. I thought I was just doing mundane tasks. I didn't know God was developing a potential star volleyball mom.

Isn't that just how God works in our lives? We feel like we are going through the motions, not really accomplishing much, but God has bigger plans. He uses every good thing we do, no matter how small. We must be faithful and not give up. Because one day we will reap the harvest. And like my soaring volleyball, the harvest may be higher and greater than anything we can imagine.

Dear God,

Thank You for encouraging us in scripture to stay strong and not tire of doing good. Help us realize You are developing strength in us even when we cannot see it. Amen.

Growing in *Strength*

1. Think of a time you have been discouraged and could not see what God was doing. How did God use that situation to develop strength in you?

2. What do you do when you feel weary and want to give up? How do you develop more strength?

3. How can you encourage someone who feels like giving up?

Chapter 10

Being Up for the Challenges

Battle Scars

Kristy

For I am the LORD your God who takes hold of your right hand and says to you, Do not fear; I will help you. Isaiah 41:13

A wise woman once told me, "Kristy, you can't make it through life without a few battle scars." I was a teenager at the time and didn't fully grasp the magnitude of her wisdom. Although I didn't understand it, for some reason, her words really struck a chord with me. Years later, after I'd been bruised by life's storms and acquired a few "battle scars" of my own, I realized what she meant. Life isn't always smooth sailing. Sometimes there are rough waters that can batter you, nearly causing you to drown.

I've experienced a number of challenges that left scars. For starters, I had to be removed from my mother's womb with forceps. The forceps scraped my face, which caused a minor scar. "It looks like she's already been in a fight," the doctor announced to my mom. Later, as a little girl, I fell on a sharp rock which deeply cut my forearm, leaving a scar. At age twelve, I had a bone cyst. It was biopsied and thankfully benign, but the surgery to remove the cyst left a scar. I also have a scar on my chin from a bad skateboard wreck, another from a c-section, and two from knee surgeries.

So, yes, there are physical marks. But I don't believe those are the scars the woman was talking about. She was talking about the excruciating wounds that are often invisible. The emotional scars.

Physical challenges are tough, but often the hardest challenges prove to be the ones like broken relationships, financial hardships, heartbreaks, silent illnesses, hurt feelings, bruised egos, bitter disappointments, and other painful trials. They tend to beat us up. Those brutal scars seem to take longer to heal—bcause they take more than Band-Aids or stitches to fix. They require healing from Jesus, our Great Physician. Once healed, those scars can teach us, mold us, change us, and help refine us.

The most difficult challenges—when I am hanging on by a thread, nearly drowning in the waves crashing over me—keep me turning to Jesus. My lifeboat. The struggles that have brought me to my knees in prayer have drawn me closer to Him. I've had to lean on my heavenly Father over and over again. Repeatedly, He rescues me.

Through tears, heartaches, losses, worry, stress, and frustrations, God is the one we can go to with our hurts. He is our hope, our strength, and our rescuer. He can deliver us from the challenges we endure.

As an example, I'm fortunate to have one of the good guys. We have a great, solid marriage. But around year eight, we were not experiencing much "wedded bliss." In fact, the bliss had mostly turned to arguing. He was traveling a lot for work and barely home long enough to unpack, wash clothes, sleep, repack, and leave again. The money was good, but the toll it took on our relationship was not.

We finally sought counseling. Our marriage counselor was a woman, so I thought I'd have an edge. I knew she would see my side of the story, thought we'd have some kind of "girl power" solidarity to team up against my husband. After all, he was mostly at fault, right? Only a few sessions into our counseling sessions, I learned I could not have been more wrong. It turned out she wasn't biased and didn't take sides. She did, however, help me realize how I was at fault, too—as much as, if not more than, he was.

The counseling proved valuable, and we got our marriage back on track. Mainly though, we had to call on Jesus. It took prayers, grace, and forgiveness on both sides, but we struggled through that test and came out better for it.

Challenges are difficult, but they can also help build character. With Jesus holding our right hand, He teaches us not to fear and encourages us to come to Him. He helps us. If you call on Jesus, He'll come to your aid and help pull you out of those treacherous waters. You might not escape troubles without a few battle scars, but you can certainly be rescued by our Lord. He can provide hope and healing. Because of His scars, ours are covered.

Dear Lord,

Thank You for being there for me. Life brings challenges, but it's good to know You are the lifeboat coming to my rescue. I praise You for helping me overcome the troubles I face. I'm grateful for Your healing power. Amen.

Overcoming *Challenges*

1. What has been your most difficult challenge?

2. How did you overcome it? Did you turn to Jesus?

3. In what ways have you experienced God's rescue and healing from life's trials?

Life Rains

Sue

Give thanks in all circumstances; for this is God's will for you in Christ Jesus. 1 Thessalonians 5:18

In the past few years, I've learned to embrace the good, the bad, the ugly, and the awesome. Life brings them all. It's not easy. I would much rather choose only the good and the awesome, but life doesn't work that way. I began to notice I felt off balance when I didn't include the bad and ugly as part of the whole. Through trials, tribulations, prayer, and lots of therapy, I found ways to accept them. Now before you say, "Bravo Sue," understand it continues to be a process for me. I did discover, though, when *life rains* get in the way, embracing them all provides a magical balance when storms abound.

There are all kinds of rain. The kind that pitter patters on our roof on a cloudy day. Softly tinkling on the windowpanes, creating a drowsy melody that can lull us to sleep. Then there are those swift, angry rains that twist with the wind, pounding us, leaving red welts that sting. Some are heavy downpours, lasting for hours. Drenching everything in sight. They have the ability to cause massive flooding and leave long-lasting damage. Yet even others have a gentleness about them. Like the soft rain which provides a much-needed drink to the thirsty ground.

Challenges in life present themselves in the same way. There are those that we welcome. A bit uncomfortable when they present themselves, but we trust and know we can get through them. They even make us feel a bit better as we grow through to the other side.

Some struggles hurt physically and emotionally, sometimes leaving scars.

Then there are the ones we think will never end. These keep us up at night and cause havoc on our heart and in our mind.

Finally, the ones that are filled with age-old trust. We know we have been here before and realize we will be better and stronger because of them, accepting that this too shall pass.

Rain is necessary. Without it, growth doesn't happen. Time spent planting would be in vain. Fruit trees would not bear fruit. Flowers would grow deep looking for sustenance and their blooms would never reach for the sky. Grass would shrivel up and lose its color. Rivers would not flow, and wells would dry up.

Challenges are necessary, too. They are part of the stories of our life. They stretch us. They provide much needed wisdom. More than anything, they show us we need to depend upon our Lord for His strength. Our strength alone is not enough to sustain our lives.

Life rains come and life rains go, just like the storms themselves.

Our Father never promised there would not be storms. He did promise He would be there with us as we walked through them, and He can use them to help us truly grow.

Dear Lord,

Thank You for the rain. Thank You for being in the midst of every storm. The good ones and the scary ones. Help us to know we are not alone and that the rains will pass once again. Each and every one. You know our comings and our goings. Our hurts and our pain. You know when the winds come and when storms are upon us. Thank You, dear Lord, for carrying us through the challenges. Amen.

Overcoming *Challenges*

1. Can you think of a time when the storms were huge in your life? How can you be thankful in the midst of them, no matter what they were?

2. Deuteronomy 31:6 tells us what we need to be strong and courageous. Assuring us that God is with us. Do you need to be reminded of that today? How?

3. Can you begin to accept and be thankful for future storms and life rains? How different will your life be if you do? What will change?

Facing Challenges:
Fight or Rest?

DeAnn

Blessed is the one who perseveres under trial because, having stood the test, that person will receive the crown of life that the Lord has promised to those who love him. James 1:12

Some days, I just want to lie down on the floor and give up.

Maybe it's because of politics, protests, disagreements, social media wars, or simply being on hold with the phone company for two hours. But most of the time, I want to give up because I am exhausted. Tired of trying. Weary from failure.

Although I've struggled with pain and autoimmune disease for years, my mind cannot accept this fact, especially on January 1 of each year. Without fail, I make a list of New Year's resolutions that would be difficult, if not impossible, for a fully healthy person to complete. Never mind that I have never been successful at accomplishing even one-fourth of the list. No, this year will be different. I will finally have enough willpower to push through. I will plan meals and cook and finally make the budget balance. I will start my own business. Hallelujah!

And each year, by January 15, I am sorely disappointed. Instead of reaching my goals, I am wrapped in a blanket on the couch, in pain, thinking about what might have been.

A few years ago, I visited my mom with my little dog, Angel. Mom had a strict "no dogs in the bed" policy, so she bought a pop-up fully enclosed mesh playpen for Angel to sleep in at night. We put the dog bed inside the playpen and added a couple of bricks to make sure Angel couldn't move the pen. Then we put her in the pen and trotted upstairs to bed.

A few minutes later, we heard a thunderous noise growing closer. I ran out of my bedroom, and there was Angel bounding up the stairs—cage, bricks, and all. Somehow, she had figured out in that little dog brain of hers that she could flip the playpen sideways and run in it like a gerbil on a wheel. Not only did she figure that out, she also had the strength to run up steps, even with bricks and a cage trying to hold her down.

After I quit howling with laughter, I let Angel sleep in the bed with me. Even my mom had to revoke her "no dog" policy after witnessing all that tenacity.

What must have gone through Angel's mind? There she was—trapped, weighted down, alone in the darkness. Yet she didn't give up. Her brain came up with a plan. She wasn't burdened by her circumstances. She fought with all her strength to break free, and she did.

Angel didn't lie down on the floor and surrender, like I want to do. She accepted the challenge and battled. I think the Lord encourages us to do this as well. In Joshua 1:9, we are reminded to be bold because the Lord is with us. "Have I not commanded you? Be strong and courageous. Do not be afraid; do not be discouraged, for the LORD your God will be with you wherever you go."

If a tiny dog with limited resources can overcome hardship, how much more likely are we to prevail with the Lord fighting with us?

I often replay that scenario with Angel in my head. I want to be like her, overcoming challenges by sheer force. I want to break free of the bricks that are holding me down. However, some days I can't do that. I am too weak. For example, the toughest part of having a chronic illness is knowing when to push through the pain or knowing when to stop and simply rest. I know that if I push myself beyond certain physical limitations, I will crash and pay a price with my health.

I believe this is true in facing any sort of challenge. Sometimes we can fight a physical battle with absolute determination, knowing that God is with us. Other days, the pain is too great, either physically or emotionally, and we are forced to stop. The death of a loved one, a job loss, an illness—any of these can knock us flat, and no amount of our own strength or willpower can overcome the devastation. That is okay, too. The Lord doesn't expect us to be strong and fight every battle ourselves. Often, we simply need to rest in the Lord and let

Him take over. Exodus 14:14 reminds us of this. "The LORD will fight for you; you need only to be still."

When faced with challenges, we are tempted to give up. We may feel like our dreams and goals are thwarted. We may think we are failing. However, God doesn't require us to complete a list of accomplishments. He doesn't care about New Year's resolutions. He has a specific plan for each of our lives and has promised to give us strength to carry out His plan and wisdom to let Him fight when we cannot. The important thing is that we trust Him to help us overcome any challenge. We can pick ourselves up off the floor of defeat, knowing God will provide everything we need.

Dear Lord,

We know You have promised to be with us in challenging times. Help us to rest and trust in You to provide strength for the battle. Rescue us when we are weary, and help us encourage others who are struggling, too. Amen.

Overcoming *Challenges*

1. How has God called you to actively participate in overcoming a challenge? How did God provide strength?

2. Has God helped you through a time when you could only be still? How?

3. How do you know when to fight with God's help or when to be still and let God battle for you?

Chapter 11

Resting in Amazing Grace

Weightless Grace

Kristy

For it is by grace you have been saved, through faith—and this is not from yourselves, it is the gift of God. Ephesians 2:8

I woke up to a sink full of dishes. I'd been too tired to wash them before going to bed the previous night or even put them in the dishwasher. Now that's tired. The day before had been exhausting—filled with meetings, extra work with deadlines, pulling weeds, tending to family needs, walking the dog, running errands, doing laundry, cooking, and other household chores. It seemed there just wasn't enough time in the day.

Staring at the dirty dishes brought waves of guilt. I began beating myself up—thinking that a good wife and mom would have washed those rather than let them sit overnight. Looking around the house, I judged everything needing attention. My house could use a deep cleaning. Dusty baseboards, windows with fingerprints, carpet stains—the list went on. Being a domestic diva was not my forte, and I convinced myself that most other people would've already taken care of all those household chores.

The first thing I do most mornings is have my coffee and quiet time with the Lord. So, before washing the dishes and hitting the ground running, I decided to follow through with my normal routine. I took my coffee out on our deck and refocused by praying, breathing in fresh air, and listening to the birds sing. When I went back inside to read my morning devotion, I came across the phrase written by Ann Voskamp, "Grace is weightless." Reading those three words was like a healing balm for my soul. How I needed that reminder of God's infinite grace.

God's grace erases the mistakes of yesterday. He gives us fresh starts with each breaking dawn. God sent his son, Jesus Christ, to die on the cross for our sins. The thought crossed my mind that if we don't accept God's grace, He would've died in vain. Breathing a sigh of relief, I knew I didn't have to be perfect. Maybe I should offer myself some grace, too.

I thought about all those times in my life when God extended His grace toward me. They were too numerous to count. I am nothing without God's grace.

I am so grateful for the Lord in my life. Without His grace, I wouldn't be writing this. God's grace has given me the strength to endure trials. It is a debt I cannot repay. It's too heavy. His grace is free. It is weightless. We can't earn it. We don't have to do good works to receive it. We must only accept it. It's a gift with no strings attached for sinners like me. If we accept Jesus into our hearts, we are saved by His grace.

In due time, I did get my dishes washed, my baseboards and windows cleaned, my carpets shampooed, and all my other to-do list items done. I needed to extend a little grace to myself, just as Jesus does. I encourage you to accept God's grace, appreciate His mercy, and offer yourself the same. We aren't perfect people, but we do serve a perfect Savior. Rest and relish in the freedoms of His goodness, His grace, His mercy, and His love. Love yourself and don't beat yourself up in the process. Accept the gift of His "weightless grace."

Dear Lord,

Thank You for loving me enough to give me the free, weightless gift of Your grace. I'm so grateful You wipe the slate clean, erasing my sins with Your unlimited grace, mercy, and love. Amen.

Growing in *Grace*

1. What does grace mean to you?

2. Think of a time when you experienced favor from God. How did it make you feel?

3. Do you beat yourself up and find it difficult to extend grace to yourself? If so, how can you change that?

Grace, Grace

Sue

The law was brought in so that the trespass might increase. But where sin increased, grace increased all the more.

Romans 5:20

Grace, grace, God's grace,
Grace that will pardon and cleanse within;
Grace, grace, God's grace,
Grace that is greater than all our sin.[2]

~Julia H. Johnston

---

2   Johnston, Julia H. "Grace Greater Than Our Sin." Public Domain, 1910. Accessed January 26, 2022. https://hymnary.org/text/marvelous_grace_of_our_loving_lord#Author.

Just as my body thirsts for water, my soul thirsts for grace. I sure have needed gallons of it throughout my lifetime.

When I look back at the life I've lived so far and begin adding up the times grace presented herself, I lose count. I've consumed large doses of grace from family, friends, neighbors, business associates, and countrymen of every shape and size.

Grace was bestowed upon me when I was "that" person in line at the grocery store who couldn't find her wallet. She showed up when I insisted I had sent a document to a client, only to find out that it was still in my outbox. Visits from grace occurred numerous times when my "yes, I will be there on time" turned into "oops, I thought I had more time." I can't even count the number of times I spoke without thinking, and the recipient of my words waited until I was finished and then, with grace, showed me how my thinking needed a little more attention.

Without grace, there seems to be no completion. It's kind of like an ice cream cone without the cone or a house without a roof, a song without a tune, or a pretty vase without a flower. Grace gives us the opportunity to be whole. The best that we can be.

I asked a bunch of people what came to their mind when they heard the word grace. Their answers were varied but ran in the same vein. Thanks. Forgiveness. Mercy. Undeserved. Salvation. Kindness. Unconditional love. A gift. Peace.

The one that really made me stop in my tracks, though, was *undeserved*. Isn't that the truth? I didn't deserve grace from any of the people mentioned above, and I definitely don't deserve grace from my Lord. But isn't that just like Him? To give me something He knows I need. To provide me with something that would quench my thirst. To lay out in front of me a gift so big, so beautifully wrapped with such love and care. One that I don't deserve.

Grace has followed me from year to year, town to town, and challenge to challenge. She shows up when I least expect it but always when I need her. She is one of the biggest, brightest, most colorful gifts I've ever had the pleasure of unwrapping.

There were times in my life that my children wanted and needed gifts that cost more than I had in my pocket. So I saved my money. I worked harder. I sacrificed for them.

But that was nothing like the sacrifice Jesus gave so He could surprise me with the gift of grace. It didn't come free. It was very expensive, but He knew I would need it. Not just for a moment, but for my entire lifetime. A gift that would keep on giving and would appear in front of me, asking to be unwrapped over and over.

Grace. A gift I don't deserve, with my name on it. A gift I want and need. Grace has covered every single one of my transgressions. Each one should have landed me in nothingness; but instead, by grace, I have been given an eternity of completion.

Dear Lord,

Thank You for my priceless gift. It was just what I needed. Just the right size. It fits me perfectly. You know me so well, Father. You've turned my rags into riches. Your grace is sufficient for me. Amen.

Growing in *Grace*

1. Where has grace shown up in moments of your life? Grab a sheet of paper and write them down.

2. Take a moment and imagine your life without grace. What would that look like?

3. Have you given the gift of grace lately? If not, what can you do right now to make grace the first step you take instead of the last?

Grace and the Chore Chart

DeAnn

And if by grace, then it cannot be based on works;
if it were, grace would no longer be grace.
Romans 11:6

A blank chore chart hangs on my refrigerator.

The kind you list chores on for each member of your family and then check them off throughout the day with a dry erase pen when each person completes their jobs. It is empty now because people in our household routinely "forgot" to wash the dishes or wipe the counters or dust and vacuum, and "chore enforcement" is not my talent. I eventually gave up.

About ten years ago, I decided we just needed a better system for chores. I spent quite a bit of money on The Ultimate System to hold kids accountable. It came with a book, personalized peg boards to hang little picture cards of completed chores, reward tickets, ideas for weekly family meetings, and prize ideas. We were set. Yet each week, something would come up—someone would be sick, we would stay up too late and be too tired to mop, or we would watch too many cartoons and forget to hang our clothes in the closet. Once, my son took out the trash and then asked to take a nap afterwards because "that was so much work." Obviously, we are a lethargic bunch, pretty much incapable of self-discipline.

This past year, I was determined to keep myself organized even if no one else participated. I bought The Ultimate System for home management. It had checklists for every day, with about twenty boxes to check each day for routine chores and another five for weekly chores. Guess how many I checked off this week? Six. Not per day. Six checkmarks for the entire week. Not the 175+ that I should've checked. Another fail.

For most of my life, I treated my faith like the chore charts and management systems. I was sure I could please God by checking off the right boxes—be loving, patient, forgiving; visit the sick; give to the poor; or pray for an hour a day. I still have a tendency to try this, yet always fail miserably.

What a relief it was the first time I heard about God's grace. He sent His Son to die for us as a gift. By believing and accepting that gift, the lists and charts can be thrown out the window. We don't have to earn our salvation. We can simply have faith.

"For all have sinned and fall short of the glory of God, and all are justified freely by his grace through the redemption that came by Christ Jesus" (Romans 3:23-24). Thank goodness.

We are justified by His grace and don't have to earn it on our own. Working harder or faster or completing a huge to-do list doesn't please God. We can have eternal life with Him by simply accepting the gift of His grace through His son, Jesus. What a gift!

By the way, that chore chart is magnetic and color-coded. I think it adds a certain flair to the kitchen décor, but I really leave it up because it's a symbol of hope. Even though the kids are young adults, I still have a dream that one day we will get our act together and have a perfectly organized, clean house. But even if we don't, the blank chore chart is here to stay. It's a great reminder of grace. God has already completed the work for us by sending His Son to die for our sins. We don't have to check any boxes. We can rest easy, knowing that God's grace has already filled them all.

Dear God,

I praise You for the gift of Your Son, Jesus. Thank You for sending Him to die for me. Free me from the burden of trying to please You on my own. Help me see that Your gift of grace is all I need. Amen.

Growing in *Grace*

1. What kind of rules do you try to live by to please God?

2. Do you ever resist the idea of grace? How?

3. How might you live your life differently if you fully accepted God's grace and quit trying to earn His favor through a checklist?

Chapter 12

Looking Beyond

Disappointments

In All Things

Kristy

And we know that in all things God works for the good of those who love him, who have been called according to his purpose. Romans 8:28

When I think of pageants, I automatically think of glamorous young ladies who are beautiful, smart, talented, and walk gracefully in high heels. I can barely wear a wedge heel, let alone high heels, and I don't even own mascara. Glamorous I am not. So it's hilarious I thought it was a good idea to enter a pageant. However, as a fourteen-year-old in 1981, I was a contestant in the "Easter Seal Teenage Miss" pageant. The proceeds from entry fees went to support the nonprofit Easterseals, which serves individuals with disabilities.

The funny thing is the only talent I had at the time was barely being able to twirl a baton. I also played "Fur Elise" so badly during a piano recital, my piano teacher said, "Beethoven just rolled over in his grave." Not even kidding.

Despite my lack of glam and talent, my parents didn't talk me out of my pageantry hopes and dreams. They were supportive of my decision, always my biggest cheerleaders, no matter what the endeavor.

So there I was, entering this pageant. It took a village to help me dress for the occasion. My mom, cousin Emily, and Aunt Betty took me shopping to find the perfect pageant dress. After a long day of searching, we found a light pink dress with a lace overlay. Like Julia Roberts' character Shelby in the movie *Steel Magnolias*, I like pink. It was a "signature color" kind of thing.

The pageant was held in Knoxville, Tennessee. I don't recall many other details from that night, but I do remember being backstage in the dressing room applying lipstick and using enough hairspray for three people. Back then, my brother, Bryan, would jokingly threaten to call the Environmental Protection Agency to report me because of all the hairspray I used. After all, it was the 80s. Big hair was the must-have fashion statement.

During the pageant, I remember walking across the stage doing the pageant wave. The next thing I knew, it was time to announce the winners. Along with the other contestants, I was hoping to win the competition. The announcer called the name for fourth place. Not me. Then came the third place name. Me. I won third, which looking back was quite an accomplishment, especially since I was inexperienced in the pageant arena.

Even though I came in third, I remember being disappointed it wasn't a first-place trophy. I accepted my trophy and still have it today. However, back then it was a big disappointment I didn't bring home the gold, so to speak.

Disappointments come in many forms. We can find discouragement easily. Rather than look at the negatives, though, it is better to focus on the positives. There was eventually a bright side to this story, and it's a God thing.

Eleven years after that Easterseals pageant, I picked up a brochure about a camp for individuals with special needs. It turned out to be an Easterseals camp. I happened to be studying special education at the time. When I read about this camp in Virginia, I thought it sounded perfect. I applied to be a camp counselor and got hired for the position based on my prior work with kids with learning differences.

Working at summer camp was one of the greatest experiences of my life. I have such fond memories of the camp staff made up of people from around the world—some of whom I remain friends with today. More importantly, I loved working with the children and adults who came to the camp. They impacted my life in such a remarkable way. Working alongside the Easterseals staff and campers was truly an honor and much more meaningful than a first-place trophy ever could be for me. Little did I know when I was fourteen that God was working behind the scenes to bring Easterseals into my life in a wonderful way. I'll never forget that summer camp.

If you're finding yourself discouraged by one of life's devastating blows, I encourage you to keep on keeping on. I'm confident the good Lord is working it all for good if you love Him, just as it is written in Romans.

I might not have won the pageant, but years later, I won so much more through Easterseals. I met amazing campers, gained valuable experience in the special education field, and made lasting friendships. That is a great victory—and I didn't even need high heels or hairspray to do it.

Dear Lord,

I praise You for turning my disappointments around and working behind the scenes. Thank You for bringing me through discouraging times. I'm so grateful for the experiences You give me. It is amazing seeing You bring things full circle and working all things for good. Amen.

Overcoming *Disappointments*

1. When was the last time you were discouraged?

2. How has God turned your disappointments around for good?

3. What has come full circle in your life? How did you see God in the details?

The Disappointment Cycle

Sue

Instead of your shame there shall be a double portion; instead of dishonor they shall rejoice in their lot; therefore in their land they shall possess a double portion; they shall have everlasting joy.
Isaiah 61:7 (ESV)

Disappointments. They come in all sizes and colors. There are tests I didn't pass, friends I let down, contests I didn't win, and more than anything, the times I could have tried harder.

For a long time, in my mind, disappointment, shame, and regret went hand in hand. Birds of a feather that stuck together. They all stuck to me.

Being disappointed in myself created a cycle. At a young age, I learned how to create a recording of these shortcomings in my head, laying down track after track, constantly repeating in heart-splitting dissonance how many times I had disappointed the Lord. It was a broken record playing over and over.

One day, as I was ticking off the numerous failings in my brain, I said out loud, "Father God, I'm discouraged that I've disappointed you." Oh, just the memory of that moment causes my blood pressure to rise. It was hard enough to let others down, but when I thought about how I had let my heavenly Father down, not just once, but over and over, it made me physically ill.

No sooner were the words out of my mouth than I felt a gentle hand pointing my chin upward. Immediately, my eyes were redirected from me and aimed into those of my Savior. In my selfish condemnation, I had forgotten that this is the reason the Lord sent Jesus to die for me. So my disappointments would be washed away. Replaced with joy, hope, and faithfulness.

God was talking to His daughter. Loud and true. His voice calmed me. I began to look at myself differently. No longer clothed in dirty rags of shame and regret. God had laid out a beautiful, new dress for me to put on. When I looked in the mirror, I started to have a glimpse of what God sees in me.

I began to realize my disappointments did not define me.

Yes, they were part of my story. Yes, they sat in my human memories. But God began to help me sort through them. I began a new recording. I quickly realized my successes far outweighed my failures. I was not a disappointment to my heavenly Father. I was a sinner, saved by grace, by His Son, Jesus Christ. A new song, one that gave glory to my King, was being recorded.

Dear Father,

Help me continue to see myself through Your eyes. I am trying to live a life pleasing unto You. Help me to pause and not walk into areas that would cause disappointment to You or to me. Thank You, Lord, for giving me new garments to wear and a new song to hear. You know exactly what I need when I need it. Amen.

Overcoming *Disappointments*

1. Have you forgiven yourself for your disappointments? If not, why?

2. Can you remember a time God spoke to you, reminding you of your success? What did He say?

3. When you look in the mirror, what do you see? What do you believe God sees? How are the images different?

Mom Doesn't Always Know Best

DeAnn

*Not only so, but we also glory in our sufferings,
because we know that suffering produces
perseverance; perseverance, character; and
character, hope. Romans 5:3-4*

My daughter jumped into the van after school, breathless with excitement. "Mom, I think I'm going to sign up to run for Student Body Historian." She paused, eagerly awaiting my response.

I thought for a few moments and then did what any thoughtful, encouraging mom would do. I said, "Let's not."

I usually pride myself on being an encourager, but to be honest, I was tired. This was not our first rodeo. I had helped oversee four different campaigns for our kids in the past four years. We nearly went bankrupt buying candy and making stickers and posters. But that's not why I was weary. I was tired of defeat. Our daughter lost in her two prior elections, while our son won both of his. I didn't want my girl to be disappointed again.

Not that she was a stranger to discouragement. Her dance studio closed right before her big recital. Her cross-country season ended when she ran into a fire hydrant. Her first rollerblading session resulted in a broken wrist after skating ten feet. She caught pneumonia and had to be hospitalized during her first soccer season. A trip to the orthopedic doctor revealed a diagnosis of "bowler's thumb" during her first year of bowling. I began to believe she was doomed in anything extracurricular.

And now, she was willing to run for an office that involved campaigning in the entire middle and high schools. I didn't want her to be embarrassed in front of the whole school.

Yet, somehow, she believed she could win. After much pleading and begging on her part, I finally relented and said yes. Yes, you can run. Let the flurry of speechwriting, outfit shopping, poster making, and campaign strategy begin.

On the inside, though, I struggled. "Lord, why? Why would you let such an innocent, precious soul fail? Someone who has never said an unkind word about anyone, who works around the clock, who has such a heart to please you. Why can't she succeed?"

The day of the election, my anxiety rocketed to an all-time high. I told the Lord I was turning the results over to Him, and, as much as I wanted to protect my child, I was turning her over to Him as well.

At 3:00 p.m., she came bouncing out to the van.

"I won, Mom. I won!" she yelled, with the most excitement I had seen in years.

Yes, you did, I thought, *in spite of me.*

I thought I knew best. I believed I was protecting her from further hardship and disappointment. Isn't that what we do as parents? As friends? As a family? We try to shield those we love from suffering in any form. But God showed me the truth of the words in Romans 5 during a school election. "We know that suffering produces perseverance; perseverance, character; and character, hope." Aren't character and hope what we really want for our loved ones? Or do we want to protect them at all costs and keep them from learning the lessons God is trying to teach them?

That ended up being one of the best years of my daughter's teenage life. I think all the previous failures made her victory even sweeter, and she learned to listen to God's voice instead of mine.

Mom doesn't always know best, but God does. If we let Him tell our loved ones what He wants them to do, they might just end up doing more than we ever hoped or imagined.

Dear God,

Help us when we face disappointments. Remind us of the truth of Your words, which state that You are growing something new in us—perseverance, character, and hope. Assure us of Your plan and give us strength to continue trusting You. Amen.

Overcoming *Disappointments*

1. What disappointment is holding you back in life? How?

2. Name something positive God has shown you through disappointment in the past. How has that developed perseverance, character, or hope?

3. What if you stopped trying to protect yourself and others from disappointment? What would happen if you looked at the qualities God is developing instead?

Chapter 13

Moving From Control to Complete Surrender

From Stubborn to Surrender

Kristy

Come to me, all you who are weary and burdened, and I will give you rest. Matthew 11:28

The typical definition of surrender is to stop resisting an enemy's attack and to submit to their authority. I think of surrender as waving the white flag and giving up. I don't like admitting defeat. I don't like throwing in the towel. Period. Not that I'm proud of that, but it's the plain truth. I admit it. I'm stubborn. Just ask my mom.

She knows my stubbornness well. I was so stubborn when I was a little girl that my parents have several stories about said stubbornness.

One day, when I was riding my tricycle in my grandparent's driveway, it started raining. My grandma told me to get off the trike and come inside. I refused. It rained harder. I continued to ride. Grandma had to physically pull me off the trike, at which point I hauled off and kicked her. That was not my finest moment, and I got in big trouble for not surrendering that day.

Another time, I woke up thirsty in the middle of the night and wanted some milk. Dad was kind enough to oblige and went to the kitchen to pour me a cup. He poured the milk in a big cup, but Mom always poured my drinks in a small cup. I refused to drink the milk out of the big cup, insisting that it was the wrong one. My dad said, "Well, we'll sit here until you do." It became a battle of wills. I eventually drank the milk, but we sure did sit there a long time before I surrendered.

One evening, we were visiting our next-door neighbors. When it was time to leave, I refused to put my shoes back on. It had started snowing while we were there, and I was determined to walk home barefoot in the snow. My dad ended up having to carry me home while I kicked and screamed the whole way.

Sadly, I could go on. Let's just say that I'm fairly certain I could've been the poster child for "Stubbornness."

Thankfully, I'm not as stubborn as I was during childhood, but I still have my moments. For instance, when it comes to "let go and let God," I sometimes resist the letting go part. I tend to hold on for dear life. Sometimes I still go kicking, screaming, and refusing to surrender just like when I was a little girl.

Being stubborn is often exhausting. It's usually in that place of exhaustion I find myself surrendering to the Lord. I finally turn my burdens over to Jesus, realizing they are safer in His mighty hands than in my feeble ones. Giving my troubles to the Lord is sometimes easier said than done because I like to be in control. The times when I do yield to Him, I breathe a sigh of relief, knowing He's the one ultimately in control.

At times, relinquishing control to God is a long, exhausting, drawn-out process. I sometimes wait until there is no other option. We need to remind ourselves that God isn't our last resort. He should be our first. If we surrender to Him sooner, we find the rest we need. Our burdens become light.

When I was growing up, we sang the hymn "I Surrender All" in church. At that young age, the lyrics didn't mean as much as they did when I became an adult. The longer I walked with Christ, the more those words became nourishment for my soul. When I sing the song now, the stanzas remind me I can love and trust Jesus. I can freely surrender all to Him and live in His presence, knowing everything will somehow be okay. It might not make sense; but if everything did, what would be the point of faith?

In life, we might get an unexpected medical diagnosis, receive bills we don't know how we can possibly pay, or lose a loved one in a tragic accident. Life is hard. It's when we turn those difficult situations over to God that He will carry our heavy load.

When we trust in Him, the Lord brings a peace only He can provide. It is usually our struggles and places of submission that draw us closer to Him. If we submit to our Father, who loves us more than we can imagine, we will find rest.

Dear Lord,

Thank You for loving me through my stubbornness and letting me give my burdens to You. I'm thankful You give

me much needed rest from the exhaustion I feel from
trying to do things only my way. Amen.

Growing in *Surrender*

1. Is it easy for you to give your troubles to God? Why or why not?

2. Have there been times when you were too stubborn to surrender? Please explain.

3. How do you feel after you let go and let God?

Hands Up

Sue

He must increase, but I must decrease.
John 3:30 (ESV)

One day during a church service, early in my faith journey, I saw some individuals raising their hands at worship time. They seemed to have a freedom I did not possess, each person completely uninhibited in their actions. It was like a beautiful dance between themselves and God.

After the service, I pulled one of the ladies aside and asked her to explain why she had her hands lifted high. She smiled and said, "I raise my hands in surrender. Completely surrendering my life to Jesus. Giving Him total control and releasing my own."

I never forgot that, and in time, I was able to do the same. Worshiping my Lord and relinquishing my own control. Ha, I wasn't always great at the control thing. My plans had failed time and time again.

Surrender is not a walk in the woods, though. To give up absolute control to someone else is scary. Let me tell you, it's not giving up momentarily that is hard. That's not the part that takes extraordinary strength. What takes strength is permanently letting go.

I found myself having to surrender repeatedly because I kept taking it back. I found myself in a vicious cycle: surrender, release, overwhelming fear, and then the game of "give and take back."

Have you ever been there? It's exhausting.

Learning how to let go and trust God has been a lifelong venture. Surrender involves putting up my hands, leaving myself open, uncovered, vulnerable. Sometimes it feels like walking naked in a crowd of people. I'm exposed. But that is what it takes. Opening myself up to the Lord and trusting Him unconditionally. No games. No take backs. Just surrender.

Once I do, freedom washes over me. I feel emancipated. The worry, anxiety, fear, and agitation wash off me. They are replaced with wonder, awe, amazement, and reverence. Reverence for my heavenly Father, who knew how important surrender would be in my life.

I wish surrender was my go-to. Unfortunately, the human part of me ends up knee-deep in the opposite. I must remind myself what it feels like to live in surrender to the Lord. To walk in His promises. Especially the one in Matthew 28:20, when He assures us, "Surely I am with you always, to the very end of the age." If we believe this, if we know it in our hearts, surrender becomes easier. God never leaves us, never forsakes us, is with us always, no matter what the situation.

Surrendering to Him takes the burdens off us and places them at His feet. At the cross. The place where He died for me. The place where I need to surrender all.

Dear Lord,

Help me to surrender daily. To trust You without fear. You died so I could live. So I could spend eternity with You and Your Father in heaven. Help me to let go. To not hold on to my own thoughts of fear and anxiety. Surrendering fully to You brings me comfort. Knowing You have my back makes me want to draw even closer to You. Thank You, Lord, for this gift of surrender. Amen.

Growing in *Surrender*

1. Where are you in your surrender journey? Do you trust unconditionally, or are you still caught in a repeating cycle?

2. What ways can you "surrender all" in your current situation?

3. Do you walk in complete surrender? If not, how can you make this a practice in your life?

Surrendering our Hearts

DeAnn

Trust in the LORD with all your heart
and lean not on your own understanding;
in all your ways submit to him,
and he will make your paths straight.
Proverbs 3:5-6

My husband called and said the doctor needed to talk to me. I immediately knew it was bad news.

A few days earlier, I made an announcement: we would have the best Christmas ever now that we had a baby to enjoy. That proclamation was the kiss of death. The next day, I woke up with strep throat. Two days later, I slipped going down the stairs, broke my foot, cracked my tailbone, and had surgery.

Because I was unable to move without help, my husband took our one-year-old daughter to the cardiologist without me to check out a murmur. I knew a phone call meant something terrible.

The doctor got straight to the point.

"Mrs. Starling, I'm actually surprised I am calling with this news. Your daughter looks completely healthy, but she has a very serious heart defect. She is going to need a rather difficult repair that will require open-heart surgery."

"What if she doesn't have the surgery?" I inquired.

"She will develop heart and lung damage and probably will not live past age nineteen," he stated, his tone matter-of-fact.

I couldn't believe the words I was hearing. I hoped I was hallucinating from the pain medicine. How could my world have turned completely upside down in less than a week? I went from hoping for the perfect Christmas to hoping my daughter would survive.

I spent the next several months reading every article I could find about repairing heart defects, specifically an atrioventricular septal defect. My husband and I, along with our parents, sought second opinions and hoped for non-surgical options. We visited surgeons and asked hundreds of questions.

Nine months from that fateful phone call from the cardiologist, our entire extended family traveled one thousand miles with our daughter to Boston Children's Hospital. As we prepared for the surgery, I could not wrap my mind around the fact that doctors were going to cut my daughter's chest open and stop her heart. A bypass machine would technically be pumping her blood, but I felt like she would be "dead," at least for a short time. What if her heart couldn't be fixed? What if it wouldn't restart?

How could I, as a mother, possibly hand my child, who looked perfectly healthy, over to a team of people who could kill her? What if the scans were wrong? Shouldn't I just grab her and run?

I think, in that moment, I knew how Abraham felt as he led his son, Isaac, to the altar. God told Abraham to sacrifice Isaac, and Abraham trusted God enough to follow His directions. (Genesis 22:1-19). He completely surrendered to God's plan, even if it sounded absurd. Thankfully, God spared Isaac at the last minute and praised and blessed Abraham immensely for his obedience.

As I handed my daughter to the team of surgeons, I prayed with all of my might. *Lord, help me be like Abraham. I am giving my child to You. She might live or she might die. You know what is best for her. I surrender her to Your care. I beg You for healing on this earth for her, but I ask for healing for my own heart. Give me a heart that trusts You regardless of the outcome. Amen.*

Five hours later, our daughter emerged from surgery with a perfectly repaired heart. Three days later, she ate ice cream and almost knocked over her cardiologist while running down the hall.

Now my daughter is a healthy adult, and I wonder how different our lives might be today if we had not entrusted our daughter to the care of the Lord and the surgeons He used to heal her. I wonder if she would be alive. I ponder the suffering she would have endured.

How many times have we, as short-sighted humans, refused to surrender control to God? If you are like me, you probably think you can fix problems yourself if you get the right information or listen to the "experts." Yet, no matter how we try to solve difficulties on our own, we can't see the full picture. We may cause ourselves needless suffering by refusing to surrender to the Lord and follow His leading, even when it doesn't make sense.

My husband and I often say our daughter had the broken heart, but she wasn't the only one who had heart surgery. God answered my prayers for our daughter and changed my heart as well as my husband's in the process. He taught us to trust Him even when we can't comprehend His plan this side of heaven.

We may not be in control, but we can trust the One who is.

Dear Lord,

We praise You for Your perfect plan. Help us to remember You hold our future, even when circumstances seem impossible. Grow our faith and give us the strength to surrender to You and trust You. Amen.

Growing in *Surrender*

1. What does "surrendering to God" mean to you?

2. Why do you think we are reluctant to surrender to the Lord? What steps can you take to turn more over to Him?

3. Describe a time when you avoided additional pain by trusting God.

Chapter 14

Trusting God's Plan

A Hope for My Future

Kristy

*In their hearts humans plan their course,
but the LORD establishes their steps. Proverbs 16:9*

When I started working with kids with special needs during the summer months, I didn't plan on working in that field long term. Yet I did.

When I graduated from college, I didn't plan on receiving a mental illness diagnosis. Yet I did.

When I met Ken, I didn't plan on marrying him. Yet I did.

When I was pregnant, I didn't plan on having an emergency c-section. Yet I did.

When I started writing, I didn't plan on making it a career. Yet I did.

When I was in quarantine during a pandemic, I didn't plan on writing a book about hope during a time that seemed hopeless. Yet I did. Actually, *we* did—Sue, DeAnn, and I.

The "when I was __, I didn't plan on __" moments in life are numerous. There are way too many to list, but I can look back at every one of the above scenarios and tell you exactly how God was in the details. My plans may not have turned out as I planned or expected, but they didn't catch God by surprise. Nothing does.

I often wonder how many times God has had to intervene just to get me back on the right path to be in His will. How many times have I planned my way without consulting Him, only to find my plans were entirely wrong for my life? How many times did God step in to save me when I made bad choices? Did He keep me from the consequences of my poor decision making? I know the Lord isn't like a Fairy Godmother who waves a magic wand and makes our lives perfect. No way. However, I know God cares about us so much that He protects us.

One summer when I was a teenager, my family was packed and ready to go on vacation, but oddly enough, none of our cars would start the day we planned to leave. It was strange. There were minor issues wrong with each one of them. For instance, one had a dead battery. Because of the car troubles, we had to leave a day later than originally planned. We wondered if God was preventing us from being in a bad wreck or something. Did He step in?

Our plans may change or fail. However, God never changes. He never fails. Jeremiah 29:11 assures us that God knows the plans He has for us. They are plans to give us hope and a future. Do we really believe that, or are they just words on a page? Do we believe He has plans to prosper us and not harm us? If we do, why do we fret so much when our plans crumble? Shouldn't we trust God's plans more than our own? We often insist on white knuckling our objectives and holding on for dear life. Wouldn't our lives be so much easier if we asked God to reveal *His* plans for us?

Personally, I want to have so much faith that I don't even bat an eye when my personal itinerary doesn't work out. What about you? I imagine that kind of faith would be contagious. God has big plans for our lives, and guess what? He is a big God. Does it mean our lives will be without hardships? Of course not. It does mean, though, as I shared in Chapter 12, He is working behind the scenes for our good if we love Him (Romans 8:28).

I am a planner. I'm a list maker. I even like to have my Christmas shopping done by Thanksgiving. Relinquishing control is not something that's easy for me. I'm still a work in progress, and sometimes I just need to get out of God's way. I know His plans are solid, and He is a sovereign God. That's where I find hope for my future.

Dear Jesus,

Your master plan is awesome. It's so much better than mine. Thank You for loving me and for having detailed plans to give me hope and a future. Amen.

Growing in *Plans*

1. When your plans have gone awry, do you wonder if God interceded? How?

2. How have the objectives you had for your life turned out differently than expected?

3. Give an example of a specific time when you saw how God's plans were much better than yours.

What Plans are Made Of

Sue

Many are the plans in a person's heart, but it is the
Lord's purpose that prevails. Proverbs 19:21

Oh, the wonder of a little girl's dreams. I had plans as a young child, lots of them, in vivid technicolor. I used to sit and envision my life in a lovely forever home located deep in the country with wildlife and peaceful starry nights, surrounded by a white picket fence. A puppy. Every little girl needs a puppy to hug and cuddle. I imagined having a big family with ten of my own children. A family that consisted of both a mom and a dad. As I grew older, those dreams grew. I began to expand my list. A college degree in psychology. A knight in shining armor. And a little red Ferrari to top it all off.

As life would have it, those dreams took on a different hue.

Dad and Mom divorced when I was two and my little sister was just months old. Dad remarried and began a new life with another ready-made family. As a single parent, Mom struggled. She did her best but moved us from one abode to another. We didn't set down roots until I was around seven.

Home became a little three-room house smack-dab in the middle of an alley in the city. Not a star in the sky to be seen.

As life spun forward, those little girl dreams began to unravel. That college degree kept moving further down the line as I landed knee-deep in the world of survival. Oh, and remember that puppy? Well, puppies needed food, time, and care. Gee whiz, I could barely feed myself, let alone bring a little furry mouth into the mix. That sports car was as far away as the moon, and my knight in shining armor got real rusty, real fast.

Yes, those plans had a bit of a filter on them at the time. I couldn't see God's plans clearly, but He wasn't finished. He just had a different timeline than I did.

At nineteen, I had already lived a large life. Became an old soul pretty quickly. Poverty can do that. Then, at a large motivational event, I met my Lord head on. As life has always dealt with me, it was a dramatic display of affection that He showered down from Heaven. Met me in my pain. Met me in my shame. Met me in the midst of my chaotic plans. I was blown away that there was a God who truly loved me with all my faults and wrong-turn decisions. At that moment, my lists of plans seemed to matter less.

Some people have problems making plans. Not me. I've never had any issues when it comes to the planning process. I have one of those uber creative minds. I enjoy it. The plans just form in my head, and I run with them.

Most of my A plans have been followed by the rest of the alphabet: Plan B, Plan C, Plan D, etc. It wasn't until I settled into what God wanted for my life that I realized I needed to put a pause button on my plans. I needed to wait for His plan to take root in my life. I began to realize His plans were always better than my own. His plans were custom made for me. Once I became a mom of three daughters, not ten, God made that apparent.

When I sit outside my lovely home, surrounded by wildflowers, watching my husband make dinner on the grill, I am reminded God's plans for me were not for possessions or places, or even people. They were to show me He loves me. They were to show me how to love Him and others.

Yes, life didn't turn out the way my human brain thought it would, but I am able to clearly see that God was not surprised by one twist or turn in my life. He was with me. Holding and comforting me when my dreams didn't materialize. If I had only known. Now I'm thankful His plans prevailed.

Oh, by the way, when I was fifty-nine years old, my father came back into my life. God, in all His glory, blessed me and my sister with an earthly father whose plan A's didn't work out either. But one who had prayed for God's plan for his life to one day come to fruition.

Looking back at the way God has continually surprised me, I can now see that the colorful world of a little girl's dreams pales in comparison to the brilliant spectrum in God's plans.

Dear God,

Thank You for being there to catch me when my plans were not part of Your plan. For loving me and being

there always. For Your purpose prevailing in my life.
Amen.

Growing in *Plans*

1. What plans did you have as a child? What did you think your life would look like as you grew older?

2. Look around and make a list of how God's plans were different from the plans you made. Compare them. What did you find?

3. How can you see God's love through His plans for you?

Planning for an Award

DeAnn

*"For my thoughts are not your thoughts, neither
are your ways my ways," declares the LORD.
Isaiah 55:8*

My husband was nominated for a big award, and I could not wait to go to the fancy banquet at a hotel in Nashville. To say I was thrilled was an understatement. As a mom of two very young children, I felt like I had not left the house in years.

I spent two hours before the event trying to find a dress in my closet to accommodate my leftover pregnancy weight. I squeezed into a desperate undergarment that promised to make me look ten pounds thinner. I practiced walking in high heels again and put on my brightest lipstick. I was ready.

When we arrived at the hotel, my husband had to have his picture made with some other nominees. I was left to fend for myself at the meet-and-greet in the lobby prior to the banquet.

"What do you do?" a guy in a blue suit asked me.

I paused, not quite knowing how to answer. Should I tell him the truth? That I change diapers, fix mediocre meals, and take naps when the kids sleep?

I finally replied with, "I'm currently a stay-at-home mom to a one-year-old and a five-year-old."

I had not fully completed my sentence when his gaze drifted to the person behind me. He politely excused himself, and I moved to the businessman next to him. But a funny thing kept happening. Before I could even halfway finish my sentence, the person I was talking to would look unimpressed and move to find someone in the room with different credentials.

I upped my game. The next guy who asked me about my career got a more impressive answer from my employment prior to having children. "I graduated from Vanderbilt Law School and have practiced law in a local firm and a government agency." For a moment, I could tell he thought I was someone important; but as soon as I mentioned staying home with my children, he moved right on to someone else. In a room of movers and shakers, I had become invisible.

I entered the banquet room defeated. To make matters worse, my husband had to sit at the front of the room with the other nominees, and the only seat available for me was at a table in the very back corner, shoved up against an exit.

At a table that seemed designated for the unimportant, I sat next to Mary. I hesitated to even introduce myself at this point. But Mary was different. She started telling me she was a volunteer at a mental health agency. She was sweet and caring, unlike so many I had encountered earlier in the lobby.

"I used to be a lot like the people here," she confided. "I had an important job with a major company, but then I was diagnosed with schizophrenia. Now I live in a group home where I have help with my medications, and I can't work."

As Mary poured out more of her story, I tried to encourage her and told her what an inspiration she was. I could tell she was hungry for someone to listen, and I was more than happy to be her audience.

After our dinner, the lights were dimmed, and all the nominees were called to the stage, one by one, to stand in the spotlight. They all had such long lists of accomplishments. The more I listened to their achievements, the worse I felt about myself. *Lord, I am so sorry. I should've worked harder, stayed in the workforce, done more to make You proud. I bet You are so disappointed in me. I should be on that stage. I don't know what happened. Forgive me.*

As I sat there wiping away tears of defeat in that darkened room, I heard the Lord say, "If I were in that room, do you think I would be up on that stage?"

"No, Lord," I replied.

"Then where would I be?" He asked.

"Probably in the back of the room helping or serving someone," I replied.

"Exactly," He said. "I would be in the back corner talking to someone like Mary. Don't you see? *Today I let you sit where I would have been.*"

How many times in life have I made plans to accomplish something I think will impress someone? Or even God? Yet God continually reminds me my ways are not His ways. He can use me, and you, in the back corners, in our messy homes, with our crying children, or in our tiny office cubicles. He's not wanting to be impressed. He just needs us to be open to any call to love and serve the people around us.

In 1 Peter 5:6, Peter says to "Humble yourselves, therefore, under God's mighty hand, that he may lift you up in due time." The day I felt the most humbled, I received the greatest blessing.

I can't even remember if my husband won the award all those years ago, but I vividly recall the Lord giving me the most distinguished honor of doing His work that day. And I didn't even need any credentials to do it.

Dear Lord,

Thank You for the plans You have for us. Teach us to seek Your will instead of the praise of others. Help us to show Your love by serving and loving others. Amen.

Growing in *Plans*

1. What plans have you made that never materialized? How did that make you feel?

2. How have you dealt with disappointment from failed plans? What scriptures might help you deal with those disappointments?

3. What has God taught you about His plans?

Chapter 15

Knowing the Prince of

Peace

Peace from My Everlasting Father

Kristy

*Peace I leave with you; my peace I give you. I do
not give to you as the world gives. Do not let your
hearts be troubled and do not be afraid.*
John 14:27

I was raised in the boondocks of an East Tennessee town. We lived
on a winding country road, and one day as I was riding the bus
home from school, I saw an unfamiliar car sitting out in front of our

house as we rounded a curve. Right beside the car stood my dad, beaming with pride. It was nearing my sixteenth birthday, and he'd bought me a car. It was an older model Ford Mustang, and it had a cool factor. It was candy apple red with a white top, leather interior, and a great stereo. When I got off the bus, he handed me the keys. To say I was thrilled would be an understatement. I couldn't believe the car was mine. I thanked him with a big hug.

I drove that car the remainder of high school and throughout college. I stayed on the go and put many miles on that old car. Every time I went home from college for a visit, Dad always checked the tire pressure and oil and made sure everything was running okay. He tinkered on the car a lot. He'd bought it for about fifteen hundred bucks but joked he could've bought me a brand-new Mercedes-Benz for all the money he'd put in the repair work to keep it running. Most people remember their first car, and I remember mine fondly. The fact that Dad picked it out made it even more special.

I was a daddy's girl—even as an adult. Only now I'll no longer see Dad this side of heaven. He died in 2010 after a tough battle with pancreatic cancer. When the doctor told him to go home and get his affairs in order, Dad replied with, "But you're not in charge." Dad knew God was in control. He lived several months past the expiration date the doctor had given him. He was a fighter.

My husband, son, and I lived about four hours away from Mom and Dad. One night, as my husband, Ken, was on his way home from a business trip, Mom called to tell me Dad was declining. As soon as Ken got home that evening, we headed to East Tennessee. The moment we pulled into my parents' driveway, I knew Dad was gone. I just knew it. When I walked in, I was greeted by a close family friend who gently broke the news.

Mom and her friends were waiting for the funeral home personnel to retrieve his body. I walked in the living room where he was, and as morbid as this might sound, even though my dad was dead, I crawled onto his hospice bed and gave him a final hug goodbye. His body was still warm. In what should have been one of the saddest moments of my life, there was such peace. I was heartbroken but felt peaceful at the same time knowing my father was no longer suffering.

Now, every time I go visit Mom, we spend a lot of time in the living room where my dad passed away. You'd think it might have an eerie feeling, but it is actually the opposite. It feels so peaceful. I felt the sweet presence of the Lord the night he passed, and I still feel His presence today.

Before Dad died, we knew, unless God had a miracle healing planned for him here on earth, he was nearing the end. We began making plans for when he passed. He knew I had written his eulogy, and he asked me to read it to him. I'll tell you, reading a eulogy to the person who is still alive is really weird. After he heard it, Dad said, "You've got me sounding like a saint. You tell them I was no saint, but I always tried." At his celebration of life service, I honored Dad's wishes and prefaced the tribute with what he'd told me. After the service, numerous people came up to me and told story after story about what a positive impact he'd had on their lives. It was amazing.

My dad was a truck driver and had received safe driving awards, including one for safely driving three million miles. Quite the feat. He worked hard to provide for us. He wasn't perfect, but we knew he loved his family and was proud of us.

He had a great personality and a wonderful sense of humor, but some of the last words Dad said to me were certainly no joke. He was sincere when he said, "If there's ever been an angel on this earth, I believe it's your mother." I couldn't agree more. Mom was the most patient with my father and some of his ways, and she was an ultimate prayer warrior who believed my dad could change. Sure enough, God did a miraculous work in his life over the years. I miss my dad dearly, but I'm at peace knowing he's in his heavenly home.

Losing loved ones is hard. Sometimes the pain is unbearable, but we must remember God has not brought us this far just to abandon us. I might not have my earthly dad with me, but I do have my Everlasting Father who is the Prince of Peace (Isaiah 9:6). He will comfort and love us. He can mend our broken hearts, delivering a peace that only He can.

May you feel His peace today.

Dear Lord,

Thank You for the peace that surpasses all understanding. In the midst of our earthly hurts, You are always there to comfort our hearts. I'm grateful for Your love and care. I praise You Father. Amen.

Growing in *Peace*

1. Have you lost a close loved one? Did you feel God's presence during that time?

2. Name an occasion when God gave you a big dose of His peace.

3. In what ways has God mended your broken heart and comforted you?

Seeking a Peaceful Day

Sue

You will keep him in perfect peace,
Whose mind is stayed on You,
Because he trusts in You. Isaiah 26:3 (NKJV)

I've sought perfect peace my entire life. My existence has been wrapped around this desire.

Growing up, my family was poor. The kind of poor that comes with a quest to survive. As the child of a single mom, I learned survival tactics from an early age. My childhood was frenetic. We were always trying to make the proverbial ends meet. Many times, we fell short. By the age of five, I had been diagnosed with stomach ulcers. Anxiety and fear were part of my daily diet.

A habit formed. Taking that lack of peace into my teens and adulthood built a restless spirit deep within my soul. I was always waiting for the sky to fall. And fall it did. Many times. No rest for the weary. Peace seemed like an unreachable goal.

I sought peace of mind more than anything. If I could just calm my mind. The literal translation of this phrase is "rest of my spirit." Those two words, rest and peace, seemed to go hand in hand.

It took me many years to realize peace was not a thing that just happened. Peace came through action. I was used to action. It claimed my ever-waking hours. But obtaining peace involved a different kind of action.

According to Isaiah 26:3, God will keep us in "perfect peace" if our minds are "stayed" on Him. Meaning our minds depend on Him, concentrate on Him, and trust in Him. This is action-oriented. It's so much easier to sit back in our lazy chairs of life and put self in place instead of God. That sure didn't work very well for me. Peace never followed self. As a matter of fact, chaos did.

As I matured in my faith, I discovered peace in drawing closer to my Lord through prayer and reading my Bible. By taking these actions, my beliefs were strengthened. I began believing in Him without conditions. I developed what I refer to as "replacement therapy." Replacing what caused my un-peace with the opposite. When I became anxious and doubtful, I replaced these thoughts with the certainty of God's promises. If my thoughts were anxious, I sought calming verses. Then, when fear knocked, God's peace was alive within me.

I've heard peace described as "freedom from disturbance." My thoughts had been disturbed for so many years. Tranquility was way out of my reach. But as peace began to enter my mind more and more and all else slowly dissipated, my actions turned to reaching for the One who has that perfect peace. I knew where to find the cure.

I've never claimed to have all the answers, but I know the One who does. I know I can go to God in prayer and can find comfort. Peace is just a couple of pages away. God and His Word are the greatest guides to peace.

Dear Father,

Your peace is such an amazing gift. One that allows me to walk closer with You. When my mind is clear and "stayed" on You, there is no room for anything which takes me far away. Thank You, Lord. Peace is such a sweet sound. It provides a way for me to be calm. To slide into Your arms and rest. Amen.

Growing in *Peace*

1. If you take an honest look, is your mind "stayed" on God? If not, how can you take action to keep your mind on God?

2. What scriptures guide you to peace?

3. What does trusting God mean to you?

Finding Peace Outside the Loop

DeAnn

*I have told you these things, so that in me you
may have peace. In this world you will have
trouble. But take heart. I have overcome the world.
John 16:33*

"Mom! My brother said he's going to tell all my friends I'm mean." My ten-year-old daughter yelled downstairs.

"She took all my trains. She is mean!" My six-year-old son replied.

Which brought the retort from my daughter, "Well, I'm going to tell all your friends that you are selfish."

These words, or something similar, echoed through our house from time to time when the kids were young. I always had the same reply. "Is this helpful or hurtful?"

I had read the strategy in a parenting magazine. The kids would have to answer if their words were helpful or hurtful and explain why. It actually worked pretty well, although I was on the receiving end of a few huffy "It was hurtful, okay?" comments that lacked explanations.

Several years down the road, I found myself stuck deep in a rut of regret. After my father passed away, I kept second-guessing every move made prior to his death. Replaying every decision, each medication, and every consultation with the doctors. What if I had made different decisions? Why didn't I take him to a different specialist or hospital? What if he had been diagnosed earlier? Would he still be alive? The questions were agonizing.

A few years later, I was trapped in the same cycle after making the heartbreaking decision to put our beloved family dog, Angel, to sleep. She had suffered for nearly a year with Cushing's disease, seizures, and heart failure. Our family made that final tough decision one morning when she had four seizures. Immediately afterwards, the "what ifs" began. Had I made a mistake? What if we had taken her to a better emergency vet? Could she have lived longer?

My friends and co-writers, Kristy and Sue, met me one day for lunch to lend their support. I confessed to them that I couldn't let go of the guilt. Sue suggested I might be caught in an unhealthy "loop" of regret. She drew a picture of a loop showing Fear of Doing the Wrong Thing, leading to Sadness, then Anxiety, and finally, Second

Guessing. She asked if I was stuck in an endless loop and needed to break it. I could go through the loop once, but then I had to let go. Kristy reminded me God wanted me to have peace and not be stuck doubting myself. I could trust God's timing and ultimate plan.

Then I remembered my own words from years ago. "Are these words helpful or hurtful?" Could I apply that question to my thoughts as well? I could, and the answer was a resounding, "Hurtful."

Neither my dad nor my dog would want me to spend my days torturing myself with these thoughts. The Lord surely would not. In fact, my thoughts were hurtful to Him too because I was not trusting His Plan.

During this time of doubt, I found much comfort in the book of Job. Chapter 14, verse 5 says, "A person's days are determined; you have decreed the number of his months and have set limits he cannot exceed." God knew the number of days my dad would live, and nothing I could have done would have changed that. He also knew exactly how long our little dog would live.

When you go through trials in this life and begin to doubt yourself, you can ask the same question of your thoughts—is this helpful or hurtful? God doesn't want you to live in the loop of regret. Let's trust His Plan and gladly receive the peace He alone can offer.

Dear Lord,

Help us to trust You when we tend to question ourselves. Erase our doubts and fears and replace them with a sense of Your peace. Teach us to encourage others who are struggling to find peace as well. Amen.

Growing in *Peace*

1. When have you found yourself caught in the loop of regret or negative thinking?

2. What verses can you memorize to help combat this way of thinking? What verses remind you of God's peace?

3. How can we support others in their seasons of doubt?

Afterword

As we come to the end of this book, we pray you are encouraged. You may have reached the end of our stories, but not the end of hope. Our ultimate hope lies in knowing we will go to heaven to be with Jesus and leave the troubles of this world behind.

If you would like to go further in knowing the Source of our hope, Jesus Christ, you can follow these simple steps from the Bible.

1. Know that you are loved. God loves you more than you can ever imagine. So much, in fact, that He sent His Son Jesus Christ to die so you could spend eternity with Him. Nothing you have done or will do can ever change His love for you.

    For God so loved the world that he gave his one and only son, that whoever believes in him shall not perish but have everlasting life. John 3:16

2. Believe that God has a plan for your life and that you are an important part of His bigger story. Jesus said,

The thief comes only to steal and kill and destroy; I have come that they may have life, and have it to the full. John 10:10

He desires for you to have a complete life full of purpose.

3. Realize we have all fallen short of God's perfect standard of holiness. We have all sinned.

    For all have sinned and fall short of the glory of God. Romans 3:23

4. Know that the result of sin is separation from God, but He offers us the gift of forgiveness through his Son, Jesus Christ. We no longer have to be separated from God. Through faith in Jesus, we can have a relationship with God and live with Him forever.

    For the wages of sin is death, but the gift of God is eternal life in Christ Jesus our Lord. Romans 6:23

    But God demonstrates his own love for us in this: While we were still sinners, Christ died for us. Romans 5:8

5. Believe Jesus Christ died for our sins, so that we may be saved and have eternal life after we die through faith in Him.

    If you declare with your mouth, "Jesus is Lord," and believe in your heart that God raised him from the dead, you will be saved. Romans 10:9

6. Ask for and receive God's forgiveness. This is nothing we can earn. We are saved by God's grace when we have faith in Jesus.

For it is by grace you have been saved, through faith—and this is not from yourselves, it is the gift of God—not by works, so that no one can boast.
Ephesians 2:8-9

7. Turn from your old way of life to a new life of hope in Jesus.

Therefore, there is now no condemnation for those who are in Christ Jesus. Romans 8:1

Salvation Prayer

Jesus, thank You for loving me so much. I admit that I am a sinner. I have fallen short, and I need You. I ask for Your forgiveness. I believe You died on the cross for me. You took on my sins, so I could be saved and spend eternity in heaven. I invite You into my heart, and I confess You are now the Lord of my life. Amen.

If you earnestly prayed this prayer, welcome to the family of Christ. May you continue to experience Jesus in a powerful way as you keep your faith and trust in Him. With Him, there is always **HOPE**.

Acknowledgments

From Kristy

To my husband, Ken—you are my rock. I'm grateful God gave me you. Thanks for being in my corner, cheering me on, dreaming with me, and for your willingness to go on back road adventures together. To our son, Zac—you make me proud. Thanks for being a voice of reason and a sounding board. You are wise beyond your years. You also give the best hugs in the world, for which I am thankful. To the ones who welcomed me into your family, Bob and Donna Ensor—thanks for your love and respect. I hope you feel mine in return. I'm grateful for both of you. To my brother, Bryan Townsend—you're the best little brother a girl could have. You were one of my first friends, and I'm glad we remain close. Thank you for having my back and always being there for me. To my parents, Katie Townsend and the late Paul "Peanut" Townsend—words cannot express how much I love and appreciate you both. Mom, thanks for all your encouragement and support through the years. Thank you especially for being a role model and teaching me about the love of Jesus. Without Jesus, I wouldn't be standing. Dad, thank you for teaching me that I can do anything I set my mind to. Look, Dad. We have a book. I know you're smiling down from heaven.

From Sue

To my husband 2.0, God took our lemons and made the sweetest of lemonade. Keith, I love living life sipping it with you. Mama, I feel your smile every day. You continually inspired me to give my smile to others who didn't have one of their own. To my three lovelies, Amber, Sarah, and Julia, who have encouraged me, lifted me up, and believed in me. I love you too, pok, I love you more. To my sis, Patti, and partner in chaos, you are my bestest friend in the entire universe. Always there, sisters forever. Jeremy, my stalwart son-in-law. Your respect, love, and encouragement have always spurred me forward. To my blessing children—Jon Kyle, Jameson, and Caroline. God expanded my heart and opened a huge space just for the three of you. My dearest grand-littles, Micah Rae, Lily Rose, and Charlotte Joy, it's my prayer that you will love to read, just like your Mimi, and then spin a story or two with a pen of your own. To every single friend, client, neighbor, and countryman I've met along my journey, thanks for being a part of my life stories. Last, but never least, my daddy. We missed a lifetime together, but then God in all His majesty spun me around, and you appeared again. Just like in my fairytales. God gave us a second chance. Thank you, my heavenly Daddy, my Lord, for giving me the ability to write, to love, and, most of all, to forgive. You sure must love me a lot.

From DeAnn

To my husband, Tom, who is the true comedian of the family. Thank you for encouraging my dreams, enduring my bad cooking and marathon napping, and making me laugh every day. You model grace to me and are still my prince after all these years. To my children, Sidney and Will, for providing me with material for this book and giving me my favorite job as a mom. I am so proud of all your accomplishments and the people you have become. You both motivate me to be a better person. To my mother, Sidney Boutwell. I can never repay all your love and support. You model what it means to be a Christ-like servant every day. I hope to one day be the kind of mom you have always been. In memory of my father, Everette Boutwell. I still want to pick up the phone to tell you every new thing your grandchildren do. Thank you for teaching me about Jesus and fulfilling your role as my earthly father so well, I have a clear picture of our heavenly Father's love. I hope this book makes you and Mom proud. To my in-laws, Bill and Marie Starling, for raising a giving, wonderful son. To my Facebook friends who first suggested that I write a book. Thank you for believing in me when I didn't believe in myself. You are the reason I ever seriously considered writing. I finally did it, ten years later.

***

Above all, thank You, Jesus, for bringing us together and giving us the hope we have in You. Thank you to our extended families and encouraging friends who supported us on this journey. A shout out goes to the Southern Christian Writers Conference and fellow writer, Melissa Hanberry, for connecting us. A special thanks to our literary team—Macey Howell and Jason Jones. We appreciate your taking a chance on us and your kindness and dedication to this project. A big thank you also goes out to the Bold Vision Books family—George Porter, Karen Porter, Rhonda Rhea, and Kaley Rhea. Thanks for believing in our little book of hope. Last but certainly not least, thank you, readers. We're glad you are here.

In Hope,

~Kristy, Sue, and DeAnn

a.k.a. *The Crooked Crown Writing Society*

Meet the Authors

Kristy Ensor is a wife, mom, writer, Jesus girl, and small-town traveler with a sense of wanderlust. She's known among friends as "The Back Road Diva," a nickname given by her husband due to her love for traveling off the beaten path. She has a BA in communications (journalism) and studied special education. Kristy has worked in various roles assisting children and adults with autism and other learning differences. Individuals with special needs teach her beautiful lessons about patience, perseverance, and unconditional love. A champion for mental wellness, she was a recipient of the Clifford Beers Award from Mental Health America of the MidSouth for improving attitudes toward people with mental illness. When not working, you can find her spending time with family, having coffee with friends, or planning her next road trip. She lives south of Nashville with her family, sweet dog, and a few houseplants growing wildly out of control. Kristy strives to offer hope, comfort, and encouragement through her writing and in her everyday life. Visit **kristyensor.com** to learn more.

Sue Mohr is a wife, mama, sister, friend, and creative road-maker. She is the founder of *The Inner Vizion*, a coaching and consulting firm serving creatives and entrepreneurs through a whole-istic approach focusing on mental, emotional, and business wellness. Sue's goal is to co-create with others, helping them find their true passion and vision. She sits in the role of Executive Consultant for a Christian TV show located in Franklin, TN, is an award-winning scriptwriter, and has directed music videos and TV episodes. Her newest venture is co-hosting a business podcast called *2 of a Kind*. Sue is an ordained minister with a desire to serve others with God's Word and is a sought-after speaker and teacher. She also leads Bible studies and writes and teaches a self-penned curriculum for women 50+ entitled *Fifty-Ness*. Digging deep into God's word is one of her favorite activities. She states, though, emphatically, that the proudest accomplishment to date has been being a mama and grandma to three daughters, three blessing children, three grand-littles, and two furry grand-puppies. She and her husband, Keith, love living in their little peaceful town of Spring Hill, Tennessee. Laughter is an important part of her daily sustenance. She strives to uplift, motivate, and encourage a 'can-do' attitude. You can find her doing just that with friends, family, and neighbors. More about Sue at theinnervizion.com.

DeAnn Starling is a mom, wife, daughter, attorney, and dog mom. She loves to write about finding humor, beauty, faith, and meaning in everyday life. She grew up in the small town of Laurel, Mississippi, where her love of Southern hospitality and deep friendships began. She graduated from Ole Miss with a degree in finance, although her bank balance does not reflect this knowledge. After graduating from Vanderbilt Law School, she practiced business law and disability law, advocating for those with mental illness. She also worked as a grant writer, raising funds for children with special needs. After meeting her husband, Tom, and having two children, Sidney and Will, she embarked on her most challenging job to date as a full-time homemaker and mother. DeAnn has documented her disastrous attempts at housekeeping, motherhood, and cooking on

Facebook to uplift others who are also domestically challenged. She lives outside of Nashville, Tennessee and enjoys having "talk-offs" with friends, finding a good bargain, dawdling on social media, and attempting interior design projects with mixed results. She blogs online at **thebestkindofbroken.com**.

Made in the USA
Columbia, SC
23 December 2022

74833749R00137